EVERLASTING DESIGN

More Ideas and Techniques for Dried Flowers

EVERLASTING DESIGN is the dried-flower lover's guide to creative arranging. Beautifully illustrated with more than 95 photographs and watercolors in sparkling full color, this invaluable reference book has everything one needs to know about arranging—from equipping a work space to buying materials and tools, from working with dried and fresh flowers to creating miniature arrangements. Five illustrated step-by-step sequences teach beginners a wide range of techniques and styles, providing them with the knowledge and confidence to improvise arrangements of their own design.

Not only an arranger's handbook, *EVERLASTING DESIGN* also presents information and instructions for creating pressed-flower arrangements, fragrant potpourris, and useful and decorative herb and everlastings wreaths. It includes a catalogue of 45 everlastings, rendered in lifelike watercolors, and their vital statistics: height, color, growing requirements, use in arrangements, and suggested drying methods. A comprehensive bibliography and source section of retailers and botanical associations make *EVERLASTING DESIGN* an aficionado's bible.

New York City.

EVERLASTING DESIGN

More Ideas and Techniques for Dried Flowers

Diana Penzner with Mary Forsell

Principal Photography by Tony Cenicola
Illustrations by Roman Szolkowski

Facts On File Publications
New York, New York ● Oxford, England

First published in 1987 by Facts On File Publications, Inc.
460 Park Avenue South, New York, New York 10016

Library of Congress Cataloging-in-Publication Data

Penzner, Diana.
    Everlasting design.

    Includes index.
    1. Dried flower arrangement. 2. Pressed flower
pictures. 3. Nature craft. 4. Wreaths. I. Title.
SB449.3.D7P46 1987   745.92   86-29101
ISBN 0-8160-1415-9

EVERLASTING DESIGN: *More Ideas and Techniques for Dried Flowers*
was prepared and produced by
Quarto Marketing Ltd.

Editor: Pamela Hoenig
Designer: Robert W. Kosturko
Production Manager: Karen L. Greenberg
Principal Photographer: Tony Cenicola
Illustrator: Roman Szolkowski

Typeset by BPE Graphics, Inc.
Color separations by Hong Kong Scanner Craft Company Ltd.
Printed and bound in Hong Kong by Leefung-Asco Printers Ltd.

1 2 3 4 5 6 7 8 9 10

32269

DEDICATION

To Seymour, my biggest fan and patient husband who dealt with drying flowers and forty-five arrangements in our small apartment; to Alexa, Jonathan, and Marina, for their love and interest in their mother's work; to Miss Anna and Mr. "G," my parents, two outstanding floral designers; and to Connie, my good and true friend.

ACKNOWLEDGMENTS

Sincere thanks to Charles Anzalone and the staff of the New York Horticultural Society and Jane Brennan, Elizabeth Hall, and Bruce Riggs at the New York Botanical Garden for their assistance in identifying unusual plant specimens.

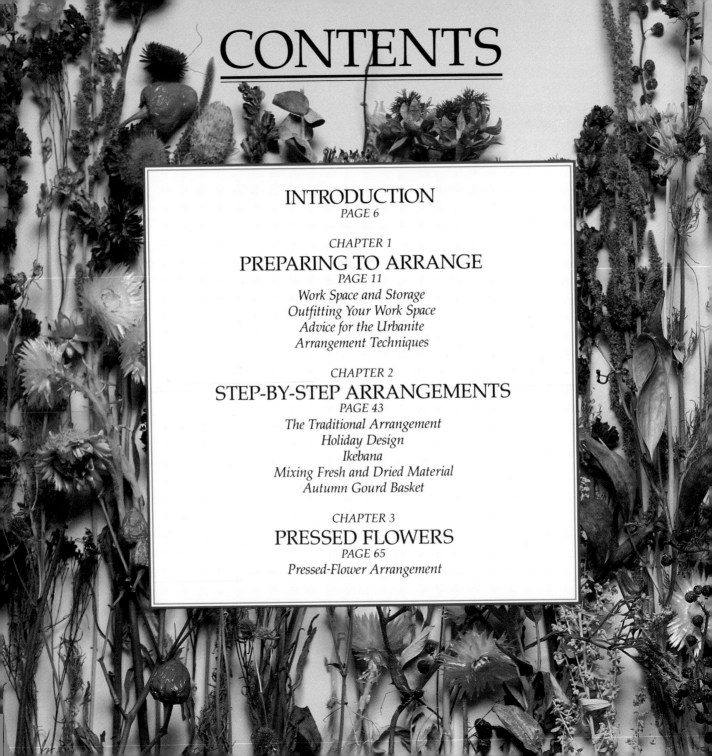

CONTENTS

INTRODUCTION
PAGE 6

CHAPTER 1
PREPARING TO ARRANGE
PAGE 11
Work Space and Storage
Outfitting Your Work Space
Advice for the Urbanite
Arrangement Techniques

CHAPTER 2
STEP-BY-STEP ARRANGEMENTS
PAGE 43
The Traditional Arrangement
Holiday Design
Ikebana
Mixing Fresh and Dried Material
Autumn Gourd Basket

CHAPTER 3
PRESSED FLOWERS
PAGE 65
Pressed-Flower Arrangement

CHAPTER 4

POTPOURRI: RECIPES AND PRESENTATION
PAGE 75

Harvesting
Preserving and Drying
Potpourri Ingredients
Displaying
Culinary Potpourri
Petal-and-Herb Potpourri

CHAPTER 5

HERB GARLANDS AND WREATHS
PAGE 87

Herb Garland
Everlasting Herb Wreath

CHAPTER 6

CATALOGUE OF MORE EVERLASTINGS
PAGE 95

AFTERWORD
PAGE 136

BIBLIOGRAPHY
PAGE 138

USEFUL ADDRESSES
PAGE 140

INDEX
PAGE 142

INTRODUCTION

I REMEMBER CLEARLY WHEN I FIRST BECAME interested in arranging dried flowers. On a crisp, beautiful fall day, I found a piece of bark that intrigued me as I was walking through Central Park in New York City. Further along I discovered pods that had fallen off a sycamore tree; these I also picked up and put into my large shoulder bag. When I returned to my apartment, I put them in my work-room, not exactly knowing how I would use them.

I soon came across other organic materials that caught my eye in my walks through the park. I loved the honey-locust pods I found because of their wonderful surfaces, which rippled with intriguing curves; the pine-cone tops that had separated from the cone when the seeds burst from the core reminded me of petrified mushrooms. My fascination increased as I became more aware of the number and variety of beautifully shaped branches, weeds, and pods that were available in city parks alone. I chose organic materials that were present in abundance, and made certain I did not harm any plants. (It is extremely important to be aware of which species are endangered before gathering in the wild, so check with your local U.S.D.A. Soil Conservation Service for a current list of protected plants.)

I had impressions of dried arrangements being, for the most part, rigid and subdued in color. I had not seen an arrangement that didn't look lifeless. However, I did recognize the enormous potential of dried material and this inspired me to design arrangements using everlastings. In working with the material I had gathered on my walks, I soon found exciting hidden colors, forms, textures, and spatial relationships that I hadn't perceived before.

The fascinating nature of dried flowers lies in the twists and turns they take in the drying process. As the stems and leaves dry, they are transformed, taking on a different visual aspect and becoming "frozen in time." Once one is aware of this natural phenomenon, one can walk through a park or the countryside with a keener sense of the beauty that nature holds. One can actually take home pieces of this beauty and fashion them into arrangements that become a part of everyday life. Country dwellers—especially those with gardens—are surrounded by this natural beauty, but even they sometimes look without seeing. City dwellers, too, are usually un-

Facing page: A delightful bouquet of ranunculus, statice, podocarpus, and Spanish moss is arranged in a simple bowl. The flowers were dried with silica gel.

Below: Sprawling rhododendron leaves are topped by clean-lined eucalyptus in this Persian brass vase. Note how the metallic color of the glycerine-treated leaves matches the hue of the container.

aware of the presence of nature around them. Even though I am an urbanite surrounded by the concrete and glass of New York City, I am still able to find many beautiful natural materials to work with in the City's parks.

The search for materials is enjoyable in itself, and as one becomes more in-volved and open to new experiences in flower arranging, creativity comes more easily. One finds a stem or a branch with precisely the curve that belongs in an envisioned arrangement, or perhaps one comes upon a leaf or weed that adds just the right touch to a particular design. These materials will hold their

Facing page: A carved gourd serves as a receptacle for bright yellow button poms and podocarpus.

Below: The unadorned beauty of protea (Banksia attenuata) needs only a complementary vase to create an attractive display. Tea set by Byron Thomas.

form and keep their beauty "everlastingly." An arrangement made from flowers gathered on a walk in the country will evoke pleasant memories of that walk each time it is looked at. This notion may sound romantic, but why do we bother to arrange flowers at all? We do because they are beautiful, intriguing, and carry with them a message of love and friendship. Imagine, for example, sending a small bouquet, arrangement, or wreath to a friend or lover with a message meant only for that person, one that will last forever.

In creating the arrangements for this book, I have tried to incorporate as much color and as many varied shapes as possible in order to introduce the reader to the fact that, along with flowers that are grown in home gardens and dried, there are also unusual and exotic imported materials from Australia, Hawaii, Holland, and many other countries. Both the country gardener and the urban dweller can purchase these materials to further enhance their arrangements. My purpose is not only to acquaint you with these flowers, but to guide you in working with them.

Once you get started in this fascinating activity you will want to find flowers that give your arrangements a personal flavor. That's the fun of it. Now let's get down to the basics of it.

CHAPTER 1

PREPARING TO ARRANGE

FROM THE MOMENT YOU BEGIN WORKING WITH dried flowers until the time you become a seasoned expert, you will always need to keep specific principles and techniques in mind when creating arrangements. When designing with flowers it is of fundamental importance to know how to confidently and efficiently manipulate your tools and plant materials. Additionally, knowing how to structure one's work space, what kind of storage containers to use, and how to proceed neatly and logically with an arrangement without cluttering the work area all contribute to the success of the arrangement. This chapter will acquaint you with basic working techniques as well as with the wide variety of materials available with which to create flower arrangements.

Container options are also discussed as are the kinds of tools you will need to have on hand. Finally, you'll be instructed in professional techniques that give an arrangement a truly unique look.

Work Space and Storage

IT'S IMPORTANT TO HAVE AN AREA OR ROOM YOU you can use just for arranging. Your work space should be kept as neat as possible, with a special place for your tools and other supplies. Put up shelves where you can store your material and containers with little worry of chipping or breakage, and, if possible, hang baskets on the wall to save space. If you live in a small apartment and do not have a separate workroom, buy only what you need to complete an arrangement; tools, floral tape, and the like can be placed in a box and stored in a closet, or in a sturdy canvas bag hung from a doorknob. Work on the kitchen counter, or, if it is too small, on the dining room table. Be sure the surface is sufficiently covered so that you don't ruin the finish of the table.

Generally, it is best to store plants horizontally, in labeled boxes, so that you know what you have in stock. You can also keep your flowers and greens in vases or glass jars; this allows you to see immediately what you have on hand (your materials may get dusty and fade a little, however). If you decide to box your own material, florists' wholesale delivery boxes—not florists' own delivery boxes—are especially good because they come in varied lengths and are deep, allowing you to store quite a lot. Large flower boxes from wholesale flower markets are also good storage containers. You should be able to pick these up from your florist or a small market that has a flower stall; florists are usually more than happy to give them away.

Be careful when packing dried flowers, as they do not have the original resiliency of fresh plants. Very delicate pieces should be wrapped in clear, lightweight plastic wrapping paper or tissue paper before they are packed away. Don't pack too many stems in one box, and remember that while you can store a number of different species together, it's not advisable to mix too many varieties, because, unfailingly, what you want will end up at the very bottom of the box.

Branches such as curly willow and pussy willow don't need to be put away with the same care as flowers. It is suggested, however, that you store them in a safe place where they can be seen but are in no danger of getting bumped into. Since branches are sculptural pieces in themselves, it's nice to display them when they aren't in use. Branches are strong, but do become brittle, so try not to stuff too many of them into one holder.

Treat commercially dried flowers very gently when unpacking them. Often they have been pushed together and become entangled, particularly if they are small flowers, so take extra care and patience with them. Do not force them apart. If you feel it is necessary, keep the stems separate by wrapping each of them in tissue paper after they've been unpacked.

Before you begin an arrangement, cover a portion of your worktable with a piece of wrapping paper; that way when the work is finished, all your debris can be easily thrown into a nearby wastepaper basket, your wrapping-paper surface ready to be used again.

When you are ready to work, have a few empty vases available that can be filled with the dried material you'll need. Large food jars serve this function well. Depending on the length of the stems, the vases and jars should be nine to twelve inches high, with mouths three to four inches in diameter so that the flowers are properly supported. Once you determine the style of the arrangement and the types of flowers, greens, or branches you are going to use, take out only as much dried material as you think you'll need. A little forethought and planning will eliminate most inconveniences and allow you to work efficiently with the least amount of handling of fragile dried materials.

After you have finished your arrangement, clean up and put everything away immediately so that you'll be ready to begin your next everlastings project.

Outfitting Your Work Space

ALTHOUGH FLOWER ARRANGING IS A CREATIVE art, it still requires planning and organization. In order to work most efficiently, you should acquire all the basic materials—from florist picks to baskets—you will need beforehand. Presented in this section are many of the possibilities for containers as well as the basic tools and materials that every everlastings designer should have.

Containers

ONE CHOOSES A CONTAINER TO COMPLEMENT AN arrangement—it should not, in most cases, be the focal point. A simple, unornamented bowl is often the best and most satisfying container to work with, as heavily decorated or vibrantly colored containers tend to eclipse the visual effect of the flower design. Containers are,

however, available in an imaginative array of sizes, shapes, and materials, allowing you to impart a unique and customized flavor to your arrangement.

Containers need not be expensive. Of course, an elegant crystal bowl does add a classic touch to an arrangement, but you might not want to use a treasured piece when there are so many other exciting, and less fragile, alternatives. You will be using messy materials such as tape and glue on your containers; therefore, reserve your best pieces for arrangements that don't require such materials. Ceramics are widely available and not expensive, and, using fibers, crafts people are creating wonderfully innovative things such as basket wall pieces, which lend themselves beautifully to arrangements.

Creating a collection of containers should be done slowly and thoughtfully. Don't go out and buy special containers when you are just beginning; rather, work with what you have on hand. Household pieces can really present a challenge to your arranging capabilities. A creamer or soup bowl, for example, can provide a surprisingly beautiful base for an arrangement. Use your imagination. Let the type of arrangement and the visual feeling you want to evoke dictate the choice of container. If you find you don't have the needed container, make an economical purchase. There are many excellent pottery stores that carry inexpensive yet attractive pieces (see Sources, page 140). Terra-cotta plant saucers are highly recommended because they are cheap, come in all different sizes, and can be painted with other colors. Thrift stores are also excellent sources of unusual containers of fine quality, and buying pieces secondhand will help immensely to keep your costs down.

Below: This nine-inch-high glass goblet holds a number of everlastings materials. Protea, palms, dill, and pussy willows are used in the arrangement; the Styrofoam base (attached to the goblet with sticky tape) is cleverly masked by Spanish moss for a natural effect. The evocative curves of the pussy willow are achieved through a bending process done while the material is still fresh (see page 34).

Above: The natural curve of grevillea provides a framework for arranging lemon leaves.

Always be on the lookout for the odd and evocative piece like the high-laced shoe on page 35. Such objects present design challenges and add to the joy and intrigue of flower arranging.

Glass

GLASS IS NOT USUALLY USED WITH DRIED flowers because, in most instances, it is transparent, allowing one to see the foam base of the arrangement. There are exceptions, however; strong materials such as bittersweet and heliconia do not require this unattractive support, and a glass vase or bowl would make an appropriate container for them. For the same reason, a container made of colored glass is a valid option if the support materials within them are sufficiently obscured.

Baskets

BASKETS ARE REASONABLY PRICED AND THERE IS no end to their shapes, sizes, unusual textures, and fiber combinations. Because they are made of natural materials, they are the traditional holders of dried flowers, the result being a harmonious marriage between two complementary mediums.

Baskets do present some problems, however. A tall basket needs weighting, otherwise it will topple. To avoid such a catastrophe, place a heavy, flat stone or a bag of pebbles or sand in the base of the basket. Another concern when working with some baskets is balance. Often, containers have traveled great distances packed loosely in big cardboard cartons. By the time they arrive at your local store, they are apt to be uneven on the bottom and slightly askew, especially if they are not well constructed. When purchasing a basket, place it on a flat surface to make sure it has an even base. Also look for unfinished ends. Check the handle to ensure it has been securely attached. If you do inadvertently buy a basket with an uneven base, hold it over a pot of steaming water and keep it there until you feel it has absorbed enough moisture (about three to five minutes, depending on the size of the basket and the flexibility of the fibers). Then, push down on the bottom of the basket with the palm of your hand. If the basket is large, place it on a hard, flat surface and push down with your palms. You will be able to tell immediately whether the fibers are responding to your touch; if they aren't, repeat the entire process from steaming to pressing until they do. Finally, set the basket on a flat surface to determine whether or not it sits evenly. (When working with small baskets, you can also use a Chinese steamer for this process, placing the basket in the steamer.)

Certain basket forms, such as the peanut-shaped basket, have an inherent balance problem, but this should not deter you from using lovely and unusually shaped baskets. To ensure that a peanut-shaped basket sits evenly, place ballast in each section; without the ballast, the basket will rock. For small baskets, use bags of pebbles or sand. For larger baskets, use rocks or oyster shells, which can be fastened to the bottom with sticky tape. No matter what type of ballast you use to steady your basket, always choose Styrofoam as your holder for everlastings and fit it in as tightly as possible over the ballast. Styrofoam is preferable to brown foam and Sahara because it comes in slab form and can be easily cut to fit the size of the basket.

Facing page: An intricately woven basket of Torrey pine needles is an ideal container for the bulbous forms of jack-o-lanterns and the delicate clusters of bittersweet. Basket: Fran Kraynek-Prince/Neil Prince

Right: This bird's-nest-shaped basket is just one of the many containers from which you can choose. The arrangement contains silica-dried daisies with their leaves and air-dried salvia held in brown foam, which is wedged into the basket.

Below: Nothing could be simpler than arranging two varieties of pine in a candle basket, which is equipped with a hook for easy hanging. The pine was placed in the basket while fresh and allowed to dry naturally. A wonderful holiday piece, this basic arrangement also allows room for experimentation: Polysilk holly with red berries attached, fresh poinsettia, dried red roses, and cedar roses can all be added to create interesting combinations of fresh, artificial, and dried material.

The natural-looking coxcomb used in this design is an
example of the effectiveness of watercolor touch-up, which
is described on pages 34–36. The ruscus was also lightly
painted with acrylic bronze.

The Oval Bowl

AN OVAL IS AN INTERESTING AND POPULAR SHAPE for a container but can also be difficult to work with. The opening is small, the inside of the bowl is large. Do not hesitate, however, to use this challenging container—it yields spectacular results. As an example of how to fit foam into an oval form, follow these instructions for the arrangement illustrated on the facing page and modify the sizes of your foam to the bowl you have chosen. For an oval bowl with the dimensions 28¾ inches in diameter lengthwise, 19½ inches at the base, and 7½ inches high:

1. Cut two pieces of Styrofoam 7½ inches long by 3½ inches wide by 2 inches high. Place a piece of sticky tape lengthwise on one piece and put the slab in the center of the bottom of the bowl. Push it down so that it adheres firmly. Repeat this process with the second piece, also placing sticky tape on the slab and placing it securely on top of the first foam insert. You will have a space of approximately 3 inches on either lengthwise side of the foam.

2. Next cut two wedges of Styrofoam, 3 inches long by 3 inches wide by 2 inches high. Place sticky tape on the bottom of each wedge and on one side of each wedge. Insert them on either side of the Styrofoam slabs already in the container. The sticky tape on the bottom of the wedges should adhere to the base of the container; the sticky tape on the sides of the wedges should adhere to the sides of the Styrofoam slabs. Be sure they are tightly wedged and do not move.

You are now ready to begin your arrangement. You'll be able to insert your stems easily into the foam, and when you are finished you'll have a lovely arrangement that looks perfectly natural without the use of Spanish moss or any other foam camouflage. This process takes patience and "stick-to-it-tiveness," but the striking results are worth absolutely every minute you spend on adapting the foam to this unique container.

Fantasy Containers

CONTAINERS NEED NOT BE THE USUAL VASE, bowl, or basket. They can also be shells, hats, and other holders that lend themselves to imaginative arrangements. Here, the principle of the container not being the focal point of the design does not apply. With unconventional containers, the flowers, foliage, branches, or other materials are an extension of the containers, bringing them to life through color, pattern, and form. You might want to use a fantasy container for a particular occasion such as a birthday party, a shower, or just because you want to do something different. Among the containers you can work with are:

shoes—high-button, pumps, ceramic, metal, and frosted- and clear-glass varieties;
dolls' heads or full dolls carrying flowers;
animals' heads or full forms (available from party and craft stores in many materials);
ceramic or paper party hats;
bags in pretty, marbleized patterns (these can also hold small vases that contain everlastings);
paper boats or fans;
stone, terra-cotta, or plastic masks.

Above: The infinitely adaptable gourd is used in a whimsical grouping in this arrangement. Small and large gooseneck gourds curve gracefully to mimic swans, their beaks created by the gourd stems. The swan gourds are attached to the main gourd by sticky tape. Flowers, greens, and Spanish moss tucked into the sides provide ample natural cover.

Left: A Greek-style stone wall mask is given a classic crown adornment of gray capucin leaves and bleached, large-leaved ruscus. Both materials are imported from Israel.

*Not all everlastings arrangements
need to juxtapose colors in order
to create visual drama. Here, a
combination of echinops and
strelitzia leaves results in a
monochromatic composition,
highlighted by the subtle hues of
the ceramic container.*

Tools of the Craft

Florists, garden-supply stores, drugstores, and hardware stores carry these items.

Wire cutters—You'll need two basic kinds: one for cutting fine- to medium-gauge wire (a Servess drop-forged cutter is recommended) and another for cutting heavy wire, such as that used in artificial flower stems (a Clauss U407 is best).

Bread knife or small saw—Either one will easily cut through Styrofoam.

Florist picks—Florist picks are small wooden pieces with wire attached to them. Available in 2½-, 3-, and 4-inch lengths, picks are used to strengthen and sometimes lengthen the stems of dried material to facilitate their insertion into foam. For the projects in this book, it's best to purchase 3-inch picks and cut them down to smaller sizes when needed. It's a good idea to sharpen picks for easier insertion into foam.

Straight wire—Many gauges of wire are available. Zero is the thickest and 30 the finest. You will be using wire ranging in gauge from 28 to 30. The wire comes in many lengths, but the 12-inch length will suit the purposes of this book.

Spool wire—This type of wire comes wound and is used for working on garlands and ordinary wiring. It is available in fine-, medium-, and heavy-gauge weights.

Fast-drying white or clear glue—Used to repair broken stems.

Spray glue—This type of glue is sprayed onto background materials to attach fabric or other coverings in pressed flower designs.

Ruler—A basic tool of arranging, the ruler provides precise measurements for foam, tape, wire, stems, ribbon, and other components added to arrangements.

Watercolors—Use these paints for touching up faded colors of everlastings.

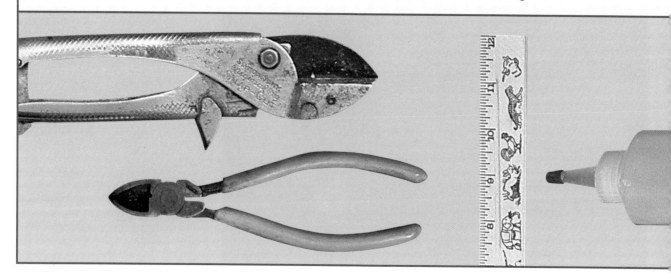

Tweezers—Buy 7-inch tweezers with a fine tip. They are useful for picking up delicate stems and maneuvering in spaces too small or awkward for fingers.

Floral tape—Very useful to the flower designer, this material comes in ½-inch-wide rolls and is made of treated paper ribbon. It is available in green, white, brown, and other colors. Your work will require the colors listed.

Sticky tape—Many arrangements in this book call for the use of sticky tape. It comes in large rolls in both white and green and is sticky on both sides. To use it, peel off the protective outer covering after the tape has been fastened to an object on one side. Sticky tape keeps Styrofoam in place in an arrangement and is also used to fasten down ornamental objects in a design.

Floral sprays—Available in many colors, these paints add bright color accents to everlastings.

Fine- and medium-sized paint brushes—Brushes are used to apply watercolors.

Polyurethane lacquer spray—A glossy coating material that will highlight and protect everlastings.

Flower preservative—This substance protects everlastings from moisture and dirt.

Glycerine—Used with branches and leaves, glycerine is a preservative.

Silica gel—This gluelike substance is used as an anchoring base for drying and storing flowers.

Cat-repellent mixture—Cats like to chew on both live and dry plants. To prevent your pet from ruining your arrangements, make up a small bouquet of materials you plan to use in a design and spray them with a cat-repellant mixture, which is available at pet stores. In this way, you can test your pet's reaction to the substance while also determining if the mixture adversely affects your plant materials.

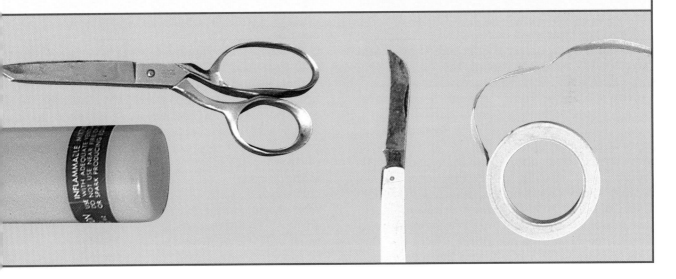

Materials for Anchoring Arrangements

THE MATERIALS YOU CHOOSE TO HOLD YOUR everlastings in place depend on your budget and the types of arrangements you wish to create. Here is a listing of your choices:

Styrofoam: The best-known and most widely used material is Styrofoam. Light green in color, it is usually available in 24-by-12-by-2-inch slabs. Since you don't want to call attention to your base, you may wish to color the Styrofoam with acrylic paints, in which case it can be sprayed black or mottled, usually with a combination of dark green or black. Sticky tape is used to adhere the Styrofoam to the base of the container.

Styrofoam is the most practical and effective material for holding arrangements, particularly those with heavier stems and branches, and works well with all silk and polysilk flowers. For slender and delicate flower stems, you will need to use picks (see page 32 for instructions).

If you are interested in using other shapes of Styrofoam, stock up on the wreath shapes and "snowballs" available during the holiday season. (As a rule, these pieces come in white.)

Brown foam or **Henry's foam:** This type of foam is available in 9-by-4-by-3-inch brick form. Brown foam is appropriate for beginners because it is softer than Styrofoam and easier to work with (it does not require the use of picks). Brown foam has to be wedged into a container because sticky tape won't adhere to its surface. If you need to hold this foam firmly in place, glue it to the base of the container, being sure to give it time to set. Do not attempt to re-use this kind of foam—it is too soft and has a tendency to crumble. Although not quite as practical as Styrofoam for working with heavy materials, brown foam is very effective for lighter stocks.

Sahara: Another option for anchoring materials is Sahara, an earth-colored material available in the same dimensions as brown foam. Although it is a denser material than brown foam, it is still easy to work with and does not require picks. As with brown foam, sticky tape will not adhere to Sahara, so glue must be used if the Sahara is not firmly wedged in a container. Once used, it cannot be recycled because of its tendency to crumble.

Bar-Fast: This moist foam is available in the standard brick form—in the same dimensions as brown foam and Sahara—and is specially sealed in a plastic bag. It recently became available in half-brick forms, which makes it a more viable purchase for the retail buyer since it is quite expensive. Bar-Fast cannot be used with glues or sticky tape, and therefore must be cut to the exact size of the container. Stems are locked in place as the material dries around them for a very firm hold. Any foam not in use must be kept in a sealed plastic bag so it will not dry out.

Kenzan: This Japanese invention is a novel way to hold dried materials in place. The loose translation of *kenzan* into English is "pin holder." A *kenzan* piece is actually a number of evenly spaced sharpened pins attached to a heavy lead base. Some models have a plastic base, but these are not recommended because of their instability. *Kenzan* models come in many forms: square, rectangular, circular, or cup-shaped, with the pins held within a concave shape, rather than directly on top of a flat surface. Using *kenzan* is challenging, for one must very carefully choose the dried material to be inserted, either directly on top of the pins or

This restrained composition is designed in the manner of Ikebana. A twisted branch and three sabrelike pods are strong vertical elements in the design. Red ruscus and a cluster of eximium scale the bases of the pods and branch. In keeping with the Oriental style of the design, the plants are arranged in a cupped kenzan *holder; small, smooth stones evoke the Japanese use of stones in meditative rock gardens; and the entire arrangement sits in a wooden Japanese candy box.*

wedged between them. A branch might be too large or too impenetrable to use or, conversely, a flower stem might be too fragile. However, flower stems can be grouped together and inserted in small bunches between the pins. A novice will have difficulty using this method, but the more experienced arranger will find it very liberating to work with because it does away with the ubiquitous Spanish moss and makes a beautifully clean presentation.

As an added word of advice, the use of foam of any kind with *kenzan* is strongly discouraged. Some people have been known to use the pin holder as a base for foam. Not only is this practice unnecessary, but it also creates problems if the pin holder is to be used for another arrangement: the foam is extremely difficult to remove from the pins.

An example of the *kenzan* approach can be found on page 25 (Japanese candy box).

Materials for
___ Camouflaging Foam ___

JUST AS YOUR OPTIONS FOR ANCHORING MATERIALS are numerous, so, too, are those for camouflaging these foams. Some of them are available in nurseries or garden-supply stores, while others can be found in gardens and parks. The following is a partial listing of the possibilities:

Spanish moss: Spanish moss is a widely used covering material that can be found growing on trees in the southern United States and the West Indies. It is classified as an epiphyte, or air plant, and is a light, easily manipulated fibrous light gray material that does a thorough and attractive job of camouflaging foam. It can be bought in both large and small quantities,

Facing page, top: A black sushi bowl is host to commercially dried delphinium in several colors as well as to glycerine-treated ruscus foliage.

Facing page, bottom: A gourd, with the stem still attached, becomes a swan with multicolor plumage. Orange-and-yellow grevillea and white statice radiate outward and back, as if windswept, and are surrounded by feathery filler.

Below: Nine different types of everlastings are integrated together in this design. The unusual purple-spiked flowers are those of the common garden artichoke. For two variations on the same basic form both natural, air-dried ruscus leaves and those which have been dyed a vivid red have been included. Protea, eucalyptus, hakea, lemon leaves, podocarpus, and sponge mushrooms are also interspersed. Because the arrangement calls for heavy materials, a Styrofoam base must be used as an anchor.

camouflaging materials, but it is an option nonetheless.

Alternatives: Galax leaves, lemon leaves, ferns, and ivy are among the other materials you can use to cover foam. Ruscus can also be used. These covering materials can be pressed or preserved by putting the stems into a combination of one-third glycerine and two-thirds warm to hot water. It takes three days or more for the foliage to drink in this concoction. The longer you leave the stems in the mixture, the darker the leaves get (a bronze color may result if the stems are left in for a long time). You can control this process and get a greener leaf by removing the material a little sooner than three days. You can determine whether or not the glycerine has been absorbed by feeling the leaves: if they are supple and slightly oily in feeling, you can remove them from the solution. Store them in a tall, cylindrical vase, being sure not to crowd in too many stems, until you need them. With the exception of galax leaves and ivy, these materials can be inserted into foam using only their strong stems. For galax leaves and ivy, use florist picks.

Advice for the Urbanite

MOST URBAN DWELLERS DON'T HAVE A CUTTING garden at their disposal and must buy the bulk of their dried material at the florist's.

In the store, dried flowers are usually rolled up in clear plastic wrapping; however, they may also be packaged in paper florist's wrapping with only the tops visible. If this is the case, it can be difficult to determine if the

but it is suggested that you buy only a small quantity at first. When Spanish moss is stored for a while, it has a tendency to dry out, and becomes tougher to pull apart.

Sphagnum moss: This moss is a frequently used covering for both fresh and dried arrangements. It is a ground cover and is generally sold in small quantities. Sphagnum moss has a tendency to dry out and disintegrate; for this reason, it is not the most highly recommended of

flowers are in good condition.

To determine the quality of the flowers before purchasing, gently turn the package upside-down. If numerous petals fall from.the package, choose another one. Although there will always be *some* droppings, a heavy fall of loose petals might indicate that the flowers have not been handled carefully.

In general, check for damaged stems and crushed, bent, or detached flowers. It's easiest to determine the condition of pods and foliage because they are usually displayed loosely in containers; any breakage or tearing will be immediately noticeable. Take your time when examining these specimens and feel free to ask your florist questions if you don't recognize the plant material. If you need further help, public botanical gardens often have services that will identify plants for you; in some circumstances there is a nominal charge.

There will be times when the florist is unable to answer your inquiries, as materials may be shipped unidentified. This is often the case with branches and greens. In fact, there are some materials used in the arrangements in this book that could not be positively identified in their dried state, regardless of whether I found them in the park or bought them at the florist.

You might prefer to dry some of your own flowers or greens. If you buy flowers for drying at a florist or green-grocer, be sure you are getting fresh stock. Flowers and greens are usually kept in clear glass vases, making it easier for you to examine the stem ends. A yellowing on the stem tips and a sort of slippery accumulation indicate that a flower is past its prime. Greens exude a musky odor when they are not fresh.

After selecting specimens for drying, snip off

Above: *Massed everlastings materials are often so beautiful that, even when not arranged in a formal design, they can provide stunning accents in the home. In this case, multicolored grevillea cascades over the sides of a dining room chair, its temporary storage place. Porcelain vessel on table: Dorothy Hafner*

Facing page: *The coppery-gold shades of dried, glycerine-treated lemon leaves echo the tones of its brass container. An attractive form of protea,* Leucodendron salignum, *is also used.*

the bottoms and place the flowers or greens in fresh, tepid water. Once they have had a drink, you will notice the flowers perking up.

When you are ready to dry your flowers or greens, choose the methods most suitable for the flowers and most convenient for you. Refer to specific sources on the topic such as *Everlastings* by Patricia Thorpe (Facts on File, 1985).

There is a continual supply of flowers suitable for drying throughout the year, since fresh flowers are shipped into urban areas from all over the world. Summertime, in particular, brings in many flowers, among them clover, daisies, German statice, liatris, delphinium, and many more plants that dry well—either by air drying or the watering method. If you take a summer seashore vacation or visit a friend with a house in the country, there are many branches, pods, and grasses that you can bring back to the city, as well as interesting seashells and small stones. Be sure to spray plants with insecticide to avoid an unwanted infestation of your apartment.

Similarly, springtime offers a vast selection of potential everlastings, among them peonies, grape hyacinth, and baby's breath. If you have a small window-box cutting garden (see facing page) or a friend with a country garden, you can use those flowers for drying. Don't harvest too many flowers at once, however, because you may not have sufficient storage space in your apartment.

In the winter, pine cones and holly abound. Many greens and branches can be treated with glycerine to keep them well preserved indefinitely (see page 28 for more information on glycerine).

Fall is the most celebrated season for plants that make lovely everlastings. Bittersweet, a colorful climbing vine with orange and scarlet seeds, is a very easy plant to dry. Hydrangea, which must be dried on the bush itself, is also available at this time of year. Tree pods fall to the ground in parks, and vines such as hops and silver lace are also ready for harvesting and drying.

In general, avoid buying fresh flowers at special times of the year such as Christmas, Valentine's Day, Easter, and Mother's Day—the increased demand makes them more expensive. Get to know when your favorite everlastings are available so that you can stock up for future use.

Natural materials from the seashore are included in this free-form sculptural design. The crevices in the shells are unconventional containers for seaside grasses, while smaller shells, starfish, and a nearby piece of driftwood also contribute to the intricacy of the design. The base of the arrangement is a plastic picture frame covered with sand-colored cotton.

A Window-Box Everlastings Garden

Whether you live in the city or country, it's possible to grow a compact, uncomplicated, practical garden just for the purpose of harvesting plants to use as everlastings. A small garden plot, terrace, or window box is all you need for such a project.

Flower arrangements in themselves, window boxes serve both practical and aesthetic purposes all year round. During the summer, one can grow flowers and herbs that can later be used as everlastings. In the fall and winter seasons, the window box can be decorated first with bittersweet and later with pine branches and cones.

The list of flowers, vines, and herbs that can be cultivated in a small-space garden is extensive. Except for all but the very largest specimens, almost anything that can be grown in a conventional garden can be grown in a limited space.

Before planting anything, assess the growing conditions in the spot you've chosen for gardening. Take note of the ratio of shade to sun and make sure that the plants you've chosen to grow are compatible with these conditions. Most nurseries and garden-supply stores will have all the necessary equipment —such as soil mixes and containers—and will also be able to help you make plant selections based on your personal needs.

If the idea of a window box seems unfeasible, you can place pots containing a variety of plants on the inside of your window ledge. Or, you may wish to hang plants indoors near a window. Growing lights will aid plant development indoors.

Container and windowsill plants need to be fertilized. Fertilizers have become highly specialized: there are kinds for flowering plants and leafy plants, as well as solid and soluble varieties that are time-released. Fertilize your plants in the spring and on through the summer, but give them a rest when fall and winter arrive. If you fertilize too much, your plants will not flower.

Plants to Grow

Here is just a partial listing of the many varieties of flowering and foliage plants that you can grow for use in your everlastings arrangements, pressed flower designs, potpourri, garlands, and wreaths. By picking and choosing among the plants below and consulting with your local nurseryman, you should be able to raise a nice selection.

Flowers

baby's breath (*Gypsophila*)
black-eyed Susans
clematis
cornflowers (bachelor's buttons)
cosmos (very delicate, press only)
daisies
fuchsia (press only)
goldenrod (air dry)
narcissus (drying agent or press)
nasturtium
pansies (drying agent or press)
sweet William

Herbs

(Do not fertilize herbs or they will not be aromatic.)

lemon verbena	rosemary
lavender	tarragon
marjoram	thyme
parsley	

Ivy

(Press only)

English ivy	Swedish ivy
grape ivy	umbrella ivy

Arrangement Techniques

MUCH PRACTICE HAS TO GO INTO THE ART OF arranging before it comes easily. Learning the techniques that turn novices into experts is therefore fundamental to your success as an arranger. Practice each technique on a few loose stems and flowers so that you'll have mastered them by the time you're ready to work on an arrangement.

Wiring Stems to Picks

TO ATTACH A PICK TO A STEM FOR INSERTION INTO foam, place the pick on the right side of the stem and wind the pick's wire around both the stem and pick twice to secure it. Holding the stem and pick in one hand and the wire in the other, wind the wire around the stem by turning the pick and stem. The wire will go around the stem and pick simultaneously. Do not use too much force; the stem might break. Practice the process on some discarded stems until you feel comfortable with it before you start working with your greens or flowers.

After you have attached the pick, cover it with floral tape to create a natural-looking blend of stem and pick. To do this, firmly place the end of the tape a little below the top of the pick; press it against the pick and pull at the same time, turning the pick in your fingers and rolling the tape toward the top of the pick. When the upper area of the pick is covered, start working down along the pick, turning the pick and pulling the floral tape. You will notice that it adheres easily to the stem and pick.

When you get down to the end of the stem, pull the tape firmly and break it off. You just pull, roll, and seal. Never go below the natural stem with the tape; if you do, you will be unable to insert the pick in the foam.

Prepare all stems that need support in this manner. Sometimes the stems of a flower are very strong and can be inserted directly into the foam without using a pick. However, be careful never to force your stems—you might very easily break a very beautiful curved piece.

Steaming

For Curves

SOMETIMES STEMS OR BRANCHES DO NOT DRY IN the manner you would like. When this is the case, steaming the stems is an effective method of achieving a natural-looking curve. You can steam everlastings in a double boiler, a vegetable steamer, or a Chinese-style food steamer.

To start, fill the steamer with about two cups of water. When the water starts to boil, turn down the heat until the water is at a simmer. Depending on the size of the flower head and the length of the stem, place two or three pieces in the steamer. Do not overcrowd—you must carefully judge how much material can be steamed simultaneously. Generally, three or four pieces are the limit. (A sizeable branch should be steamed alone.)

Allow the stems or branches to steam for three to four minutes, depending on their resistance. A flower stem is obviously going to steam faster than a thick branch. Continually check to see if the stem has been steamed sufficiently. If the stem responds to gentle pres-

Five exotic air-dried anthuriums snake out of their container as if charmed in this exotic arrangement. Their unusual coloration is heightened by that of the container. Raku bowl: Harvey Shadow

sure, you'll know it's ready. Stay near the steamer; the process is generally a quick one.

When the stem or branch feels soft, take it out and begin manipulating it into the curve you wish. Work quickly but gently. A flower will generally require only a soft curve, which can be accomplished quite easily. A branch may take a little more time and may even require a second steaming.

Fresh stems or branches—such as pussy willow—can be manipulated to create a curve even before they begin drying, using processes similar to those employed by Japanese flower artists in Ikebana (see below).

For Freshness

COMMERCIALLY DRIED MATERIALS OFTEN TAKE ON a flattened and dulled appearance as a result of packing. In order to restore the natural look of the material and to freshen it, try steaming it. A Chinese steamer is the most practical kind to use because it usually has two trays and a cover, making it possible to steam several stems simultaneously.

Use the basic steps described above for steaming in curves. Don't leave the steamer—you will need to check the stems frequently to see how moisture is being absorbed. If the foliage gets too wet, you will lose the whole stem (this is especially true of flowers).

Bending for Curves

TO CURVE A THICK BRANCH (A HALF INCH OR more in diameter) when it is still fresh, grip it with both hands and exert pressure with your thumbs. Keep your elbows close to your body

and gently bend with gradual force until you achieve the desired effect.

Soft-stemmed fresh plants require less force. Gently crush the part of the stem you want to bend with your fingers and slowly work the stem into the shape you want, exerting force with your fingers. Try to point the flower head upward as you bend the stem.

Painting Everlastings

AS FLOWERS AND FOLIAGE DRY, THEY LOSE THEIR fresh, brilliant colors. Fading is due in part to loss of moisture and can be remedied by hand or spray painting them with color. The floral spray employed for this purpose is available in florist-supply stores, comes in many colors, and is easy to use. The colors, however, are primaries, and subtle coloring is difficult to achieve. If too much spray is used, the entire effect of the flower arrangement can be ruined. Therefore, it is advisable to first experiment with leftover pieces that you are not including in a flower design so as not to run the risk of ruining a beautiful branch, leaf, or flower.

Strong colors like gold or black can provide vibrant accents or highlight an attractive line in an arrangement. Yellow floral spray is sometimes also appropriate, for example on the dill in the Easter palm arrangement on page 14. Remember to use floral spray cautiously—you don't want to drench the flower and completely ruin it.

There may be times when you want to give an arrangement a particularly strong color accent. On these occasions, choose one of the livelier floral spray colors such as red carnation, holiday green, and jonquil yellow.

Before you spray, ensure there is good ventilation in the room. You may even wish to wear a mask to avoid inhaling the fumes. It is also advisable to lay papers over your work surface and the surrounding area to protect against paint splatter.

Use a piece of Styrofoam to hold the flowers or branches in place while they are being treated. A wooden pick should be attached to the stem of a flower for insertion; unless the branches are very delicate, they should be inserted directly in the foam. Do not spray too many pieces at one time—it is best to work with only two or three pieces. Make sure the plants are equally covered on all sides; you may have to turn them around a little to accomplish this. To color the underside of a flower, remove it from the foam and spray it while you hold the flower away from you.

Be careful not to overspray—two or three

Above: In this arrangement the gold of the high-topped shoe is harmonized with sparkly gold-sprayed cedar roses.

Facing page: A twisted branch was the starting point of this design. To enhance the rugged look of the branch, serrated-leaved protea was added. The broader leaves of Protea banksia were included for contrast, and the thistlelike bottlebrush plant, Hystrix patula, was chosen for its wild look and vivid red color.

In this most unusual design, air-dried
eucalyptus and Heliconia rostrata *extend up and*
outward, demonstrating nature's sculptural bounty.

applications should be sufficient. Allow the spray to dry in between applications. Of course, before beginning an arrangement, make sure the spray is completely dry.

For a more complex and subtle result, however, it's best to paint the everlastings with watercolors, using an almost dry brush. There should be just enough moisture on the brush to help spread the color. The two hanging heliconia pictured at left are examples of watercolor touch-ups. It would have been folly to attempt to duplicate the naturally vibrant shades of the plant; therefore, small quantities of orange and red watercolors were mixed and lightly painted onto the dark areas of the pods. The color was then rubbed into the pods with the fingertips. The yellow tips of the pods were colored in the same manner. When an arrangement calls for a greater depth of color, a slightly heavier coating of watercolors should be applied.

To give the heliconia an even greater vibrancy, they were sprayed with a high-gloss polyurethane lacquer. The end result is evident: the heliconia look more alive, without appearing brash or unnatural. Although one cannot imitate nature, one can create a different kind of beauty that receives equal attention in an arrangement.

Using Smaller Pieces

AFTER CREATING SEVERAL EVERLASTINGS ARrangements, you will find you have various small pieces left over—stems, flower heads, tiny flowers with stems, and small bits of foliage. If these pieces are still in good condition they can be put to use in a variety of interesting and imaginative ways.

The arranger should set aside a box labeled "for miniature use/extra help" for such small pieces. Sturdy leftover stems can be used to lengthen shorter pieces; they can be attached with wire and covered with floral tape in the same way that picks are. Using a flower stem instead of a florist pick to lengthen a flower stem makes an arrangement look more natural.

Similarly, leftover stems can be glued onto broken-off flower stems to again create a natural-looking extension. When using this method, give the flower-and-stem joint sufficient time to dry.

Smaller flowers that are still attached to their stems can be gathered together into a miniature bouquet, which can then be wired to a pick and wrapped with floral tape. Small flowers and foliage can always be combined to form miniature arrangements that serve nicely as personalized gifts.

Broken-off flower heads can be glued to grape ivy wreaths or used in a potpourri. Small

Below, left : One of the many uses for leftover everlastings is exemplified by this amusing little arrangement incorporating Australian daisies and two red strawflowers.

Below: In this diminutive design, slightly less than one foot high, verticordia is intermingled with fragile, curved branches. Clay vase: Mary Nyburg

pieces of leftover foam can also be saved for use in miniature arrangements. Use your imagination and you'll always find opportunities to be creative with these odds and ends.

Dismantling Arrangements

IF YOU WANT TO DISMANTLE AN ARRANGEMENT, you need only perform a few simple steps. First, take all the stems out of the foam. Remember to save the pieces that still look good, setting them aside for the odds-and-ends box. Then, twist the foam from side to side; it should lift out of the container quite easily. Some pieces of foam will invariably stick to the bottom; you can either remove these with your fingers or scrape them off with a small spatula. There will be a residue of sticky tape or glue on the bottom of the container; this can be removed by pouring in a small amount of benzine and allowing the mixture to stand for a few minutes. Rub off the remaining glue or sticky tape with a paper towel; the benzine works very fast and it should come off quickly and cleanly.

Finally, wash your container with dish detergent and rinse it well. You don't want any benzine left on the surface in case you use the container for a fresh-flower arrangement.

Transporting Arrangements

SHOULD YOU WISH TO TAKE AN ARRANGEMENT to a friend, attractive paper shopping bags

Above: Bear grass streams over the sides of the shallow container of this arrangement, creating a fountainlike effect. Sprays of pink delphinium echo the flow of the bear grass, while yellow and white freesia and pink minicarnations—both dried in silica gel—provide bright spots of color.

Facing page: The upwardly curved form of a brass-and-copper pitcher complements the vertical orientation of the buckthorn it contains. The buckthorn is treated with high-gloss polyurethane lacquer, which is sprayed on. The lacquer adds gloss to the berries and secures them on the stem.

serve well as a means of transport.

To prepare a bag, cut down the four sides so that the bag stands about four to five inches high. If you wish, punch two sets of holes directly facing each other on both sides of the bag. These holes will be threaded with ribbon to hold the bag shut.

Next, cut a piece of Styrofoam to fit the bottom of the bag. Place the arrangement on the Styrofoam and outline the circumference of its base with a pencil. Scoop out enough Styrofoam within this outline so that the arrangement can be slipped directly and securely into it.

Before placing in the bag an arrangement like that pictured below or on the facing page, carefully insert straight wires into it to prevent the bag from crushing any particularly fragile flowers, foliage, or branches that extend beyond the container.

Maneuver the arrangement in its Styrofoam holder into the bag and gently tuck pieces of tissue paper under and around the edges and over the top to protect the flowers. The tissue paper also acts as an anchor so that the arrangement will not move.

Finally, tie the bag with ribbons if the arrangement is a gift or staple it shut.

*Holiday dinners will become memorable events with the
addition of this natural centerpiece. Small and large pine
cones are balanced by sycamore pods, red-dyed linen
pods, snow-white statice, and glycerine-treated pine
needles. Polysilk holly, poinsettia flowers, ribbon, and
tree ornaments can be used as additional festive elements.
The pine cones are attached to long wooden picks by fine
spool wire.*

A variety of multitextured everlastings harmonize with the earth tones and curved form of an Arabian water jug. Incorporated in this easy-to-create yet striking arrangement are protea (the globular forms); dock; narrow and broad-leaved ruscus; gladiolus and lemon leaves; tansy (yellow flowers); wheat; safflowers (orange, tufted, thistlelike flowers); liatris (purple spikes); and corkscrew willow branches.

CHAPTER 2

STEP-BY-STEP ARRANGEMENTS

JUST AS FRESH-FLOWER ARRANGEMENTS CAN BE infinitely varied to suit specific moods and occasions throughout the year, everlastings can be arranged for every purpose imaginable. Your arrangement will not just be a transient thing of beauty; it will last through many seasons and be used again and again for different holidays, or varied and updated to suit a changing household interior. In sum, a dried-flower arrangement more than returns in beauty and utility the time and care put into it.

The five step-by-step arrangements described here vary in difficulty and can be adjusted, simplified, or elaborated upon, depending on the whim or level of skill of the flower designer. The seasonal and holiday designs are not very complicated—nor are they expensive to create. In fact, many of these arrangements can be created from "found" objects. The traditional and Ikebana designs require skill and planning, but are not prohibitively difficult for the novice. Mixing fresh and dried materials demands intuition and a strong visual sense. These arrangements will help you to develop many different flower-arranging skills while providing hours of enjoyment.

As you start to arrange flowers, you will, no doubt, make errors in placement. Be sure to have enough materials on hand (Styrofoam, brown foam, and the like) to practice and experiment with. Do not expect the impossible from yourself. Once you have learned the basics, you will be able to move on to the finer points of flower design. Remember to read the instructions carefully all the way through before you start; make sure you have all the materials and tools at hand; study the photographs; and allow yourself time to complete the arrangement in one sitting, particularly if you are creating it for a special occasion.

When designing your own arrangements, it's a good idea to work out your design before you buy materials. Choose your container in advance as well—it will influence the kinds of everlastings you put into it. For example, you would not want to put birds-of-paradise in a small bowl or casual-looking daisies in a heavy bronze container.

Don't get frustrated; work at your own speed. Sometimes an arrangement just needs time to evolve.

The Traditional Arrangement

THE PRINCIPLES OF DRIED-FLOWER AND FRESH-flower arranging are identical: attention is paid to the blending together of color, texture, and the flow of forms. All arrangements work in the same way, with framework materials setting the tone for the arrangement. Lycopodium serves that purpose in this particular piece. The flowers, statice, and lavender complement the lines of this green.

Before you begin, lay your materials in the basket to see how they will look. Move them around to different parts of the basket and note how the forms interact. For our purposes, a willow basket was used as the container, but any basket of pleasing color and texture will do. Take note of the photograph of the arrangement (page 47) to see how all the elements were worked together.

Remember that as flowers and stems dry, they twist and turn to create some very interesting shapes. When inserting materials into the foam, use these curves and flows to their best advantage, working from the center out. In the traditional arrangement, a profusion of different-sized flowers and greens is allowed to overflow the boundaries of the container, eliminating the need for Spanish moss as foam camouflage. Despite this multivariegated collage of dried materials, the arrangement looks full but not crowded.

As you are working, turn the basket periodically so that you fill each part of it equally. Step away from your work once in a while to ensure that there are no holes. Take your time; aim to create a design of evenly distributed form and content. Make sure that a sense of depth and outward motion is created as well. In the same way that a still-life painter creates depth on a canvas, the dried-flower arranger must recognize the color, texture, and compositional relationships in a three-dimensional realm.

As a final touch, you may wish to place a bow in the basket or attach it to the handle. If you decide to use the bow at the outset, remember to leave a small opening for it; otherwise you can use the bow to fill in a previously unnoticed open space. Whatever the case, a bow is a quaint touch that plays up the old-fashioned quality of the arrangement.

The instructions given here are quite specific, but you may wish to add personal touches by substituting in different flowers. Place your greens and flowers in separate tall containers in front of you so that they are visible and immediately accessible. Be sure your jars or vases have mouths wide enough to ensure that the flowers are not crowded; they should fit loosely into the containers so you can remove the stems without resistance.

Be gentle with your material; it is dried and does not have the resiliency of fresh pieces. A word of advice about German statice: before you start working with it, you might want to steam it to soften the stems so they can be more easily pulled apart (see page 32 for instructions on steaming).

Of course, you're going to make some mistakes; it's only natural. Don't be daunted, persevere, and before you know it you'll be able to arrange flowers with ease and confidence.

Materials

container: circular willow basket 2 inches high, 18 inches in diameter, with handles 9¾ inches high;
1 block of Styrofoam 24 inches long by 12 inches wide by 2 inches high;
sharp knife or small saw;
ruler;
glue (optional);
3 stems of dried lycopodium (with at least 7 individual offshoots);

1 bunch of strawflowers (approximately 10 to 14 stems), leaves removed;
1 spray of German statice (approximately 10 stems);
12 pieces of lavender.

Instructions

1. Place the foam block on top of the basket, push down, and apply firm pressure, creating an impression of the basket mouth on the block. Remove the block and trim off the excess around the impression. Because the block must fit snugly, be careful not to trim too much off the sides. There will be 2 crescent-shaped spaces left on either side of the basket because the basket is round and the foam is rectangular. To fill the spaces, cut a couple of foam wedges and place them on each side of the block to keep it from moving. Keep in mind that the block is 3 inches high and the basket only 2 inches high; as a result, the foam will extend an inch beyond the rim of the basket. Do not trim. You will need the extra inch so you can easily insert the pieces that will extend sideways beyond the rim of the basket. Be sure to allow for this extra inch of foam in every arrangement you do, no matter the shape of your basket. If you have a very large basket, you may even need to use 2 blocks. Some arrangers use glue to fasten the blocks in place. I prefer to have a good, snug fit, as this eliminates the need for glue. It's also best to avoid using glue if you think you might want to use the basket again for another purpose.

2. Consult the illustration on page 46 for the placement of the everlastings into the foam.

Left: The components of the arrangement are assembled on the work surface. Clockwise from the top are: the basket, with the Styrofoam fitted and the key areas of the container filled in; lycopodium; lavender; German statice; strawflowers; and tools (scissors, knife, and pliers).

Right: Continue filling in the areas, working from the center outward. Building on the framework of lycopodium—in the center, flanking the basket handle on both sides, and extending outward from the center areas on both sides—add strawflowers, lavender, and statice in combination.

As you work, turn the basket around so that all the areas are evenly filled. As you progress outward from the center, stagger the heights of the materials so that they become progressively shorter—by controlling the angle of their slant and how deeply they are inserted in the foam—creating a feeling of depth. Don't forget to let the materials spill over the sides to create a lovely, natural effect.

The first inserted are the lycopodium stems; these create a framework around which you can place the strawflowers and statice. The first lycopodium stem is inserted into the center of the basket and should reach 1½ to 2 inches beyond the center of the handle. A nicely curved piece of lycopodium approximately 10 inches long should be used here. The remaining lycopodium stems are inserted into the *sides* of the foam, extending approximately 3 to 4 inches beyond the edge of the basket. Insert these pieces in the following areas as illustrated in the photograph: flanking the basket handle on both sides (4 pieces); extending from the center areas on both sides (2 pieces).

3. Your flowers should be chosen to complement the curves of the lycopodium greens. Remember to slant your flowers; don't just stick them in so they stand straight up. All materials should be placed so that they are slanted outward, seeming to reach out from the center of the basket in every direction.

A strawflower approximately 7 inches long should now be placed alongside and to the right of the center stem of lycopodium; its curve should echo that of the lycopodium. Next, insert a piece of statice approximately 4 to 5 inches long in front of these 2 center stems.

4. Turn your basket around and place a strawflower, that is slightly smaller than the first, on the other side of the center piece of lycopodium. Add another, slightly shorter strawflower here, and add more statice, pieces that are approximately 4 inches in length. Continue turning the basket and working outward from the center, graduating the heights by inserting the stems more deeply into the foam base and slanting them more dramatically.

The strawflowers and statice complementing the lycopodium greens on the edges of the basket can be placed alongside the greens or even above them. Vary your format as you turn the basket so that you do not create a monotonous mirror image on either side of the center lycopodium stem. For example, the basket in the photograph uses statice and a strawflower near the left basket handle and a bud and medium-sized flower near the right basket handle. Add the lavender pieces around the basket where their spiky forms will contrast with the roundness of the flowers and the soft curves of the statice. Turn the basket as you work to ensure that you've created a balanced—but not uniform—design in terms of form as well as content. Not all materials will have the same length or form; this contributes to the visual interest of the arrangement. Tuck some flowers lower down in the arrangement and allow others to reach beyond the basket.

Remember to take your time as you work and use only small amounts of material as you go.

Holiday Design

ALTHOUGH THIS LOVELY LITTLE SLEIGH WORKS well as a holiday centerpiece for an intimate Christmas dinner, it also makes for a delightful accent on a coffee table, side table, or mantelpiece, and can be given as a very personal holiday gift that can be brought out year after year.

The dimensions of your container probably

won't replicate those of the sleigh used in this arrangement, so adjust the dimensions of your foam and the amount of materials you use accordingly.

Pearly white everlastings—the name of the holiday flower used in this arrangement—grow two, three, or sometimes even four blossoms to a stalk. For the most part, these flowers are quite strong and can be inserted directly into the foam. There will be some flowers, however, that need to be glued or wired to a pick for insertion. Although the linen-pod stems look fragile, they too are resilient and are inserted into the foam in small bouquets held together by wire. Examine your flowers carefully and select them for their gracefulness and luster. Note that you will be inserting the flowers on a slant, creating a backward flow that gives the arrangement a feeling of movement (see photograph on page 51).

Materials

sleigh: 4 inches long from front to back at the base, 6 inches long from front to back at the top, 2 inches wide, 1 inch deep at the front, and 3½ inches deep at the back;
1 block of brown foam 9 inches long by 4 inches wide by 3 inches high;
fine-gauge spool wire;
6 to 8 three-inch florist picks, cut down to 1½ inches;
white floral tape;
fast-setting clear glue;
wire cutter or clipper (for cutting everlastings);
florist's knife or good pen knife;
quarter-inch wide, 30-inch length of red ribbon per each bow desired (each 30-inch length should then be cut into two pieces, one 24 inches long and the other 6 inches long);
ruler;
scissors;
2 bunches of pearly white everlastings;
1 bunch of green linen pods;
2 to 3 stems of polysilk holly with red plastic berries attached;
6 to 10 small pine cones, preferably prewired.

Instructions

1. Two pieces of brown foam should be inserted into the sleigh, one a base piece running its full length, the other a wedge-shaped piece that is stacked on top of the base piece and only extends from the middle to the back of the sleigh. The base piece should fit tightly in the container and the wedge is attached with glue. To cut the first block, press the 3-inch side against the top of the sleigh to get an impression. Trim around the impression and then cut it down to match the height of the sleigh. In this case the wedge will be 4 inches long by 2 inches wide by 2 inches high. Fit the piece into the bottom of the sleigh.

2. Cut a wedge from the remaining foam pieces. The wedge used here is 3 inches long by 2 inches wide by 3½ inches high. The wedge must slant down to the front of the sleigh, so, on an angle, cut the brown foam so that the front of the wedge is ¾ of an inch high. Glue the wedge to the top of the base and allow it to set. While waiting, you can prepare your flowers, pods, and pine cones.

3. Break off clusters of 2 or 3 everlastings. If possible, include some unopened buds in

Right: *The sleigh is shown lying on its side to illustrate the placement of the two wedges of brown foam: one runs along the bottom and the other is stacked on it in the back. Surrounding the sleigh are the tools and dried materials used to create the design. Running clockwise from the top are: florist's picks, linen pods, pearly white everlastings, ruler, ribbon, scissors, a knife, wire cutters, pliers, tape, wired pine cones, glue, and holly.*

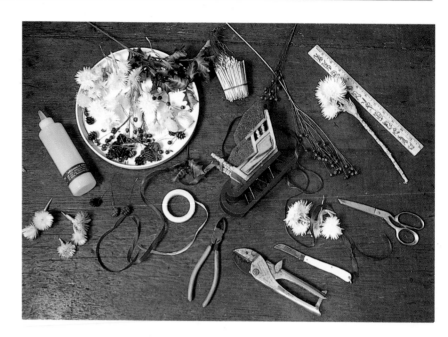

Left: *Begin this holiday design by inserting the everlastings into the key areas of the sleigh. Place them in the back, at a backward slant; to either side of the sleigh, pointing outward, left and right; and in the front of the sleigh, slanting outward over the edges. Begin filling out the sleigh by adding holly leaves with berries to the left and pine cones to the right of the sleigh. As you continue working, intersperse linen pods, more everlastings, pine cones, and holly in varying combinations throughout the arrangement.*

*The final result is a charming sleigh overflowing with a
profusion of white everlastings contrasted against the
vivid green of holly and linen pods, the woody brown of
the pine cones, and the cheerful holiday red of the ribbon.*

your clusters. If a velvety fuzz covers the stems, carefully scrape it off; this makes insertion easier. If the stems are weak, either glue or wire them to a pick (see page 32 for instructions) and cover the joint carefully with white floral tape. Before inserting the pick into the foam, sharpen its end with a knife to facilitate insertion. Cut the picks down to 1½-inch lengths so they won't take up too much room in the foam. Then set the everlastings aside for a moment.

4. Make 3 or 4 little bouquets of green linen pods, using 2 or 3 stems in each bouquet, depending on the number of pods on each stem. Wind fine spool wire around the stems to hold them together, making sure not to use too much wire. Continue winding the wire down to the end of the stems so that you are left with a sharp end to insert into the foam. Set the bouquets aside.

5. Cut the polysilk holly leaves off the main stems. A good amount of stem will still be left on the leaves. Since these stems generally have wires inside of them, they can be very easily inserted in the brown foam. Set these aside.

6. If you purchased prewired pine cones, all you have to do is attach them to a pick. If you could not find wired cones, take the fine spool wire, cut a 5-inch length, bend it over a knife to form a U-shape, and carefully slip the wire under the top petals of each cone. Twist the wire to secure it to the cone. Make several small bouquets using cones of varying sizes and bind them together with a small amount of fine wire. Attach them to a pick cut down to 1½ inches and use a small

amount of floral tape to camouflage the wire.

7. Now you are ready to begin inserting materials into the sleigh. Refer to the first photograph to see the general areas where material is added first. The back area of the sleigh is filled with everlastings, as are the left and right front edges of the wedge. Make sure the everlastings are inserted at a backward slant. The center of the front of the sleigh also gets a group of everlastings.

8. Holly leaves with berries are then added to the left back side of the sleigh. The right back side balances the design with the insertion of pine cones. Place another group of pine cones at the front of the sleigh, in the very center.

9. Work in green linen pods at your discretion. Complement the pine cones in the front with linen-pod stems pointed toward the back of the sleigh. Add an additional linen-pod bouquet near the pine cones, pointing it forward. Add an additional bouquet to the left side of the sleigh as well.

10. Fill in the center of the lower and upper levels of the sleigh with the last of the everlastings. Add more pine cones and holly at your discretion, lining the upper and lower levels of the sleigh.

11. Finally, you may insert 2 little bows on the right side and front of the sleigh. To make each bow, take a 24-inch piece of ribbon and loop it back and forth 5 or 6 times. Then take a 6-inch piece of ribbon and tie this around the center of the loops. Make a knot. Cut a piece of wire and thread it through the

back of the bow under the knot. Turn the wire down and twist it tightly so that you have formed a stem for the bow that can be inserted into the foam.

Ikebana

IN THE SIXTH CENTURY A.D., SHOKOTU, SON OF A Japanese prince, journeyed to China on a cultural tour. There he became acquainted with the methods of Chinese flower arranging, which mirrored the Chinese philosophy and way of life. He became so entranced by this art that he spread its philosophy in his own country, where it took root and eventually developed into what we today call Ikebana. There are so many styles, forms, and schools of Ikebana that students could spend a lifetime learning the many different techniques. The most basic method represents the fundamental relationship of the universe: the relative positions of the earth, man, and heaven are represented in the heights, shapes, and sweeping motions of the flowers used in the arrangement. In a limited space such as this it is impossible to explain the many manifestations of this pure and elegant style; however, much has been written about Ikebana and there are reference books available that can provide the interested reader with historic information as well as detailed instructions (see bibliography). It is hoped that the simple arrangement presented here will give you a taste of the serene sense and aesthetic enjoyment that one derives from working in this medium.

For this Ikebana-inspired arrangement, you will combine polysilk flowers with natural dried material. Introducing artificial flowers to your everlasting design will add another di-mension to your flower-arranging capabilities. The everlastings used here are curly willow branches, sometimes known as "contorted" willow. The branches are available in both long and short lengths; here you will be using the shorter pieces. When choosing branches, look for those that have interesting forms but at the same time are not too delicate or brittle. The snaking, sweeping forms of the willow provide a perfect complement to the clean, fluid curves of the polysilk irises.

Materials

container: 7½-inch diameter, ½-inch deep, green cracked-glass bowl (you can use a ceramic, metal, plastic, or china bowl as long as it has a similar shape and depth and you adjust the proportions of the Styrofoam accordingly);
1 block of Styrofoam;
sticky tape;
bread knife;
heavy wire cutter (Clauss U407 is preferable);
ruler;
28-gauge wire (optional);
3 polysilk irises, standard length 20 inches;
2 curly willow branches;
1 small bag of Spanish moss.

Instructions

1. Cut a piece of Styrofoam 3 inches wide by 3 inches long by 2 inches high. Contour the corners of the foam to create a smooth-sided natural effect. Place it in the bowl to check the fit. If satisfactory, cut a 2½-inch piece of sticky tape and attach it to the bottom of the foam. Place the foam, sticky tape side down, in the center of the container and press to be sure the tape adheres firmly to both the foam and the container's bottom.

2. Cut the first iris to a length of 19 inches, the second to 17 inches, and the third to 13 inches. These cuts should be made well below the leaves. Each of these 3 flowers should have only 2 leaves.

3. Insert the 19-inch iris into the back area of the Styrofoam, centering it right to left. The stem should stand straight in the foam.

4. Insert the 17-inch iris in front of the first iris, toward the center of the foam. Do not place it too close to the first.

5. Insert the 13-inch iris directly in front of the other two at an evenly spaced interval. The arrangement should project the uncrowded look of naturally growing flowers.

6. Now that the irises are in place, manipulate the curves of the stems so that the flowers have a more lifelike appearance.

After fitting a Styrofoam piece with contoured corners into the container, insert the tallest, 19-inch polysilk iris into the back of the container. The second, 17-inch iris is then placed directly in front of the first, in the center of the foam. The third, 13-inch iris is positioned in the front, at an evenly spaced interval.

Gently bend the 13-inch iris toward you and slightly to the right; the 17-inch iris should be bent on a slightly leftward slant; the 19-inch iris should remain centered with a slight curve to the right. As you are arranging the flowers, adjust the leaves in a complementary fashion. Check the photograph at left to see how the leaves should be contoured.

7. Cover the foam with Spanish moss. Pull the moss apart and lay it around the base, tucking it between the stems so that it looks as natural as possible. If you feel the moss needs to be further secured, cut two or three 3-inch long pieces of wire. Bend them over a knife to form a U-shape and insert.

8. The final step is to add the curly willow to the arrangement. Since your willow pieces will not exactly duplicate the curves of the branches used here, the choice and placement of the pieces are left up to your discretion. Try to choose gracefully curved pieces with approximately 3 small branches radiating from each stem. The branches should not be heavy; rather, they should follow the lines of the flowers and soften the linear quality of the irises. If you can't find the proper pieces

The stems and leaves are manipulated to form dramatic curves, and Spanish moss is added around the base to cover the foam. The finishing touch is two willow branches that act as stunning counterpoints to the iris leaves, stems, and flowers. The monochromatic backdrop of the matching tablecloth and wall color showcases this piece to its best advantage.

of curly willow, cut them from various branches and insert each individually into the foam so that they appear to be all of one piece. To facilitate insertion into the foam, cut off any curvatures at the ends of the branches. The 2 branches should sweep up the back of the arrangement to the left of the flowers. Consult the photograph on page 55 for clarification.

As you are working with this design, try to arrange your pieces in a fluid, interrelated fashion, so they evoke a serene, meditative mood in the observer.

Mixing Fresh and Dried Material

FRESH FLOWERS AND GREENS ACCENTED BY THE graceful curves of pussy willow give this arrangement a distinctive air. The 3 clear-glass vases line up in a rather modern-looking configuration that will be a real eye-catcher in any room. The simple white background heightens the clean, austere lines of the arrangement, which echo one another in each progressive vase, and the curved lines of the pussy willow serve to visually unite the vases.

Fresh, straight-lined minigladiolas and campanulas create an upward flow in the first 2 vases. In the third vase, however, the campanula merges with the pussy willow. The variation in the size and placement of the spider mums and pittosporum adds another visually interesting tier to the design.

The vases used here are all 7½ inches high, but you can use smaller or larger vases if you adjust the amount of dried and fresh material

and glass marbles used. Other flowers can be substituted, as well, but keep in mind that they should be similar in form. For example, spiked flowers such as liatris and delphinium can replace the tall flowers. A round flower such as the gerbera daisy or tulip can replace the spider mum. Greens such as the lemon leaf, ruscus, or a cutting from a variegated philodendron vine or English ivy plant can be substituted for pittosporum.

It's important that you remove the leaves that fall below the waterline from all fresh materials. This is necessary to avoid decay, which can produce bacteria harmful to the flowers.

Also vital to the successful outcome of the arrangement is the curving of the pussy willow —the sole dried material used in the design. To ensure you're getting the supplest material possible, it's best to purchase pussy willow in the spring when it is freshest and most responsive to bending.

A fresh- and dried-material mixture is a rewarding alternative to working in just one of these mediums. The arrangement's inherent appeal and visual complexity result from both the merging and simultaneous contrasting of the plants' different botanical states.

Materials

containers; 3 clear-glass vases, 7½ inches high, 2 inches in diameter;
48 glass marbles;
Floralife (for freshness, sugar or aspirin can be substituted);
florist's knife or sharp pen knife;
branch cutter;
ruler;
3 fresh, pink minigladiolas, 21 inches tall

This triadic design requires careful positioning of the materials among the marbles. Keep a large vase filled with water to the side of the arrangement so that you can easily select material from it as you work your way from vase to vase. Complete one design at a time in each container, first placing the pussy willow, then the minigladiola, followed by the campanula, and finishing with the spider mums and the pittosporum.

In the final arrangement, each vase will possess a distinctive feature that makes it different from the other two—whether it's the size of the flowers or the positioning and curvature of the blooms, leaves, and stems—but will also visually integrate with the other vases. A unified design is created by this interrelation of materials.

(one with at least 3 flowers, another with 2 flowers, and a third with 1 flower), lower leaves removed;

3 fresh, blue campanulas, 19 inches tall, lower leaves removed;

9 fresh, white spider mums (3 small, 3 medium, 3 large), lower leaves removed;

1 branch (3 stems) of fresh pittosporum;

1 branch (3 stems) of pussy willow, 24 to 25 inches long.

Instructions

1. Cut no more than a ¼ inch off the end of each flower. Make the cut on a slant.

2. Place 16 marbles in each vase.

3. Fill each vase a little more than half full with water. Add the flower preservative Floralife as per package instructions or use a pinch of sugar or an aspirin to help preserve the freshness of the flowers.

4. Curve all the pussy willow branches to match the ones in the photographs. Use the method for bending materials described on page 34.

5. In the first vase, position a curved branch of pussy willow according to the photograph on page 57. The pussy willow should be curved, with a slightly convex swoop to the right. Be sure the branch sits securely among the marbles.

6. Place the 3-flower minigladiola directly in front of the pussy willow. It should reach to approximately 3 inches below the tip of the pussy willow. Place a stalk of campanula to the left side of the minigladiola. The flower should be 2 inches shorter than the minigladiola.

7. To determine placement of the spider mums, hold each one at the edge of the surface of your worktable and cut it to the desired length. The photographs will give you an idea of how they are placed in the container. Vary the sizes and heights. The first spider mum placed in the vase should be the tallest. The remaining 2 should be progressively shorter.

8. Tuck a small branch of pittosporum to the left of the last spider mum inserted.

9. In the second vase, repeat the same steps for adding flowers. The gladiola here should have 2 flowers. The willow should also be bent to the right, but the curve should be slightly more concave.

10. In the third vase, repeat the same steps, with a convex curve on the willow. The third gladiola should have 1 flower. The campanula should follow the line of the willow.

Autumn Gourd Basket

HERE IS AN ARRANGEMENT OF MANY CONTRASTS that is simple to create because it does not require the use of complicated techniques. However, it is also a difficult piece to complete because it is a loose, free-form arrangement that requires intuitive placement of its diverse components. To create an interesting and decorative piece, you must understand how the many colors, textures, and forms of the pieces interrelate.

Among the materials used here are gourds, autumn leaves, and strawflowers. Many of the pieces were left over from other arrangements (such as broken-off strawflower heads too small to use on picks), while others were pieces I had simply collected and saved.

In this arrangement, a flat, round basket is used to openly display the material. Indian corn presides at the center, propped up by a piece of foam so that it rises above the other materials. The honey-locust pods in the upper-right area provide a sweeping, flowing form that is echoed by the wheat sprays, corn husks, and amaranthus (purple spikes). Interesting touches are provided by the furled, flowerlike golden mushrooms and the textured and smooth gourds. Yellow and red oak leaves, golden morrison flowers, and multicolored strawflowers add vibrant touches of color; green leaves lend the arrangement a welcome burst of freshness.

This arrangement can be used as a centerpiece or placed on a sideboard. Although the design obviously evokes images of autumn, the materials can be adapted to complement any season or situation. During the holiday season, pine cones can be substituted for gourds, polysilk or fresh holly or pine sprays can be used instead of wheat, and pearly white everlastings can take the place of strawflowers. Dyed and decorated eggs can be combined with curled palm for Easter, or just to celebrate springtime. For other seasons and occasions, use this basic arrangement as a starting point from which you can endlessly vary materials to create an appropriate and original design.

Clockwise from bottom left are the many components that are incorporated in this autumn design: golden mushrooms, two different varieties of wheat, amaranthus (purple), lemon leaves, golden morrison clusters, crookneck gourds, strawflowers, crown and warty gourds, tools (scissors, wire cutters, two knives), and a small block of Styrofoam. In the basket, clockwise from the top, are: honey-locust pods, red and yellow oak leaves, Indian corn, along with more lemon leaves, pods, corn, and amaranthus.

Materials

container: 1 low, flat basket, plate, or bowl, approximately 16½ inches in diameter;
clippers or scissors (to cut materials);
1 large kitchen knife and 1 pen knife (to cut and trim Styrofoam);
1 slab of Styrofoam;
sticky tape;
2 stalks of Indian corn (husks pulled back with kernels exposed);
8 gourds (2 large and 4 small crookneck, 1 of the crown and 1 of the warty variety);
3 golden mushrooms (preattached to slender 3-inch picks);
5 to 6 amaranthus stems, 8 to 9 inches long;
2 clusters of golden morrison;
10 multicolored and single-color strawflowers;
3 honey-locust pods;
3 stalks of orange-dyed wheat, 10 inches long;
3 stalks of honey-beige colored wheat, 10 inches long;
7 red and 7 yellow oak leaves;
2 branches of lemon leaves (2 to 3 leaves on one branch, 3 to 4 on the other).

Instructions

1. Cut 2 pieces of Styrofoam approximately 2 inches square by 1½ inches high. Anchor the pieces to the center of the basket, plate, or bowl using sticky tape.

2. Place sticky tape on the underside of the corn and arrange it on top of the Styrofoam as illustrated in the photograph at left. The corn should lie diagonally across the basket, the 2 stalks forming a slight V shape. This positioning establishes the orientation of the other materials in the arrangement. The corn is the focal point, and everything else seems to radiate outward from it.

3. Next add the gourds and scatter them around the corn. You may arrange them loosely or attach them with sticky tape, especially in the case of the crookneck gourds. The gourds should extend outward around the corn like spokes of a wheel. The crown and warty varieties sit atop the other gourds where their interesting textures can be shown off. The warty gourd is prominently positioned in front of the corn; the crown gourd is to the left of the corn.

4. The golden mushrooms can be tucked into the arrangement, in this case in front of the corn and to the right of the warty gourd.

5. Place the amaranthus spikes in the upper left side of the arrangement and allow their graceful linear forms to extend beyond the perimeter of the container.

6. Break off clusters of golden morrison—the small yellow flowers—and add some just below the amaranthus on the left side of the basket, following the line of the purple spikes. Add more flowers radiating frontward to the right of the corn. Also tuck some into the front area of the container, between the warty gourd and the mushrooms.

7. Place the strawflowers between the crown and warty gourds. Also position them slightly to the right of the mushrooms. In the

The completed arrangement has a casual, loose look, like a cornucopia in a flat basket. The corn is the focal point, the gourds radiating from it. Honey-locust pods sweep out of the right-hand area and amaranthus, the left. In the front lower right, wheat fans out to create a graceful autumnal spray. The other elements add colorful textural highlights all around the container.

photograph, yellow strawflowers are used on the left side of the arrangement and multi-colored flowers on the right.

8. The honey-locust pods should twist and curl elegantly from the upper right area of the arrangement. These visually intriguing forms should extend well beyond and above the perimeter of the container. If you find it difficult to hold them in place, add sticky tape to the base of each pod. You probably won't need the tape, however, as the pods will be tucked in under other materials and held firmly in place. Together, the pods should form a triadic shape.

9. Now insert the different varieties of wheat so that they run along the right side of the container. The sprays should point front-ward and fan out over the side of the container. Adjust the placement of the sprays so that some extend further out than others.

10. The red and yellow oak leaves are scattered along the front and back edges of the left side of the container. They should look like a kind of frilly trim.

11. The green lemon leaves complete the design. Add the 2 branches to the back left side of the arrangement extending outward at different angles so that 1 cluster of leaves interlocks with the yellow oak leaves to form a kind of backdrop while the other cluster complements the line of the amaranthus extending beyond the container's edge.

Remember that the materials are oriented outward from the center. They should spill over the edges to create a casual yet well-balanced design.

CHAPTER 3

PRESSED FLOWERS

WHEN ONE THINKS OF PRESSED-FLOWER DESIGN, one thinks of genteel Victorian ladies with lace at wrist and neck delicately arranging violets, pansies, and other tender blossoms on a variety of backgrounds. For most people, the extent of their involvement in this medium has been to put flowers from bouquets or corsages into a book—only to forget about and then rediscover them years later. For some people, however, pressed plants act as daily reminders of past events. My father, for example, carried for years a four-leaf clover that he had found when walking through a park with my mother before they were married.

The art of pressing flowers is over three hundred years old. It first came into being when a botanist invented the method to preserve his plant specimens. Today the art of pressed-flower design is being revived in a singularly modern way: the vast variety of flowers available in today's marketplace along with the many new and exciting materials and

This lovely illium arrangement always reminds me of lollipops. The illium are mounted on samples of straw wallpaper and their flowers and stems have been lightly painted with watercolors to heighten their color.

methods for framing pressed plants has opened up a new world of possibilities. The pressed-flower process has blossomed into a veritable decorative art form of one-dimensional flower arrangement. It has become so popular that the covers of commercially sold diaries, greeting cards, and address books often contain dried-flower arrangements.

You can use pressed flowers to create a special greeting for a friend by employing the "language of flowers" (see the boxed copy on pages 68 and 69). To do this, press a small flower or charming little leaf and insert it into a card. Not only can such a gesture highlight the written message of the card, it can also create a special message of its own that doesn't require words. To learn the full vocabulary of flowers, consult such useful specialized sources as Louis Gruenberg's *Potpourri: The Art of Fragrance Crafting*.

Like everlastings arrangements and potpourri, the delightful pastime of pressed-flower design need not be limited by your place of residence. The suburban or country gardener only has to step outside and gather a few blossoms to get started. But the city dweller, too, can indulge in this captivating hobby by visiting a florist or nurseryman and selecting from the huge stock available. Whether you choose clovers, cosmos, daisies, baby's breath, Queen Anne's lace, or any of the other numerous varieties good for pressing, be sure the stock is fresh. The city dweller might also want to start a window-box cutting garden, raising plants like English ivy, geraniums, cosmos, daisies, a variety of ferns, and philodendrons with both variegated and solid green leaves. The number of possibilities is extensive and should be researched at a local horticultural or botanical society.

Wherever you live, remember to choose plants that are nonbulky and don't seem to retain a great deal of moisture. Orchids and gardenias, for example, are not suitable for pressing because of their fleshiness and voluminous petal formations.

Traditional pressed-flower arrangements place flowers either in a bouquet style, a symmetrical motif, or as a border. You will notice from the photographs throughout this chapter that one need not use the traditional daisy, violet, and pansy to create a successful design. In fact, it is much more interesting and challenging to work with nontraditional flowers. In this chapter, I have departed from traditionally used flowers and experimented with many unusual plants. For example, on the facing page illium is pressed and used in a rather modern-looking configuration. For the background I used two different wallpapers with dissimilar textures. The coloring of the flowers has been highlighted with watercolors. Similarly, in the design illustrated at right, found objects are used: a green called "salad of the desert" from the Ein Gedi desert in Israel and a small tree branch with an intriguing form. In the design on page 71, I created a colorful interplay between pressed flowers and a shadow puppet.

Obviously, one nice aspect of pressed arrangements is that they last for years. The illium arrangement, for example, is now two years old; the design using Queen Anne's lace is four years old. Most pressed designs will last even longer.

In this chapter you will find "how-to" instructions for pressing flowers. To help inspire you to create your own designs, you may want to look through old horticultural journals, books of still-life botanical paintings, and old nursery garden catalogues. Antique and mod-

This pressing arrangement consists of a tendrilled flower head of Queen Anne's lace and two greens, one of which is known as the "salad of the desert" (lower left). This arrangement is a good example of creating a pressing from found objects: All three pieces were collected on walks, the greens while I was in Israel. The background on this pressing is handmade paper.

Everlasting Messages

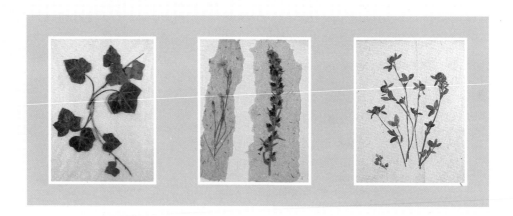

Use these plants, enclosed in cards or pressed designs, to create messages. All of these plants can be air dried, pressed, or dried in silica gel.

Flowers and Foliage

Acacia (rose, white, or yellow)	Friendship, elegance, secret love
Alyssum	Worth beyond beauty
Arborvitae	Unchanging friendship, live for me
Cactus	Warmth
Carnation (deep red or pink)	Alas, my poor heart
Clover (four-leaved white)	Be mine, think of me
Coreopsis	Always cheerful
Daisy	Innocence

Geranium (rose scented, lemon leaved)	Unexpected meeting
Ivy	Friendship, fidelity
Jonquil	Love me
Larkspur (pink, purple)	Fickleness
Lilac	First stirrings of love
Palm	Riches
Pansy	Kind thoughts
Pine (small branch)	Good-bye
Ranunculus	You radiate charm
Rose (red)	I love you
Sunflower (dwarf)	Adoration
Violet	Faithfulness
Wheat	Riches
Zinnia	Thoughts of faraway friends

Herbs and Spices

Cloves	Dignity
Coriander	Hidden worth
Marjoram	Shyness
Mint	Virtue
Parsley	Festivity
Sage	Domestic virtue
Sweet basil	Think of me

Combine these everlastings to create a message that is a charming and lasting token of friendship: small pine branch, sweet basil, forget-me-not, white clover, and red rose. This combination translates to: good-bye, wish me well, don't forget me, think of me, I love you. Try other combinations to express different feelings.

ern drawings and engraved flower designs are also potential sources of designs.

You may want to start your pressed-flower arranging on a very modest scale by simply placing a few flowers against a background that echoes the line of the central flower stem in your design, or by directly copying a traditional botanical arrangement. Because pressing flowers is an inexpensive pursuit, don't be afraid to be adventurous. Experiment with a variety of specimens. If, for instance, you purchase flowers for drying, first enjoy them fully as fresh flowers—but don't let them get *too* old or they will not press properly.

When choosing the other important elements of your pressed-flower design—the background and the frame—be sure to harmonize your selection with the dried flowers. For example, a plain-colored fabric that complements a flower is a simple yet effective choice; wallpaper textured in a straw weave also provides visual interest; handmade paper in beautiful textures and patterns is a lovely choice, but must be carefully matched with flowers. It is suggested that you choose the background to complement the pressed everlastings *after* you've practiced pressing techniques and know what specimens work best for you and will be included in your design.

Similarly, the frame must relate to the whole arrangement. Variety stores carry some very attractive frames at reasonable prices. These frames are economical with the frame, glass, and cardboard backing all provided. In the pressed-flower arrangement that follows I've chosen a plastic frame because it's easy to work with. When the work is completed, the cardboard frame is covered with a self-sealing plastic sheet and the edges are sealed with adhesive tape to make the piece airtight.

Pressed-Flower Arrangement

Materials

2 books, large and heavy enough to apply even pressure to flowers;
2 sheets of facial tissue, unpatterned and untextured paper towels, or waxed paper per the number of book pages employed in pressing;
cardboard cut to fit the dimensions of the frame;
background material (fabric, wallpaper, paper, et cetera);
frame;
white liquid or clear glue and/or glue spray;
long tweezers with a fine end;
white adhesive tape;
self-sealing plastic (from the stationery store—optional);
plain or variegated philodendron, daisies with stems cut to a ¼ inch and leaves removed (these plants are easy to begin with because they press beautifully; however, you can use anything you have on hand that you think might press well—ivy, ferns, gingko leaves, oak leaves, cosmos, Queen Anne's lace, et cetera).

Instructions

1. In an open book large enough to accommodate the plants, lay one sheet of facial tissue or waxed paper on the right-hand page and place the philodendron leaf, daisy,

This is a whimsical and unconventional arrangement, illustrating the extent to which you can improvise in this very traditional medium. In this piece I sprayed a shadow puppet with gold floral spray and paired it with small flowers of the chrysanthemum family. Because these flowers lose their vivid color when dried, I painted them with more than the usual amount of watercolor. The background material is green watered silk.

or other flower on it. You can leave the stem on the flower if it is not too heavy; otherwise, remove the stem and dry it separately. However, do leave approximately a ¼ inch of stem on the flower so it can be picked up without damaging the petals. Be sure the petals and leaves are properly arranged—once they dry, you cannot rearrange them. It's best to dry the stems and leaves of a plant separately, placing them at a distance from one another on the same page. Be sure there are no brown spots or excess moisture on the plants as this will lead to discoloration and spoilage. You should only dry one or two flowers or greens on a page at a time. Should you wish to dry more material than this in one book, place your first layer of pressing material toward the end of the book, with additional layers spaced a number of pages apart, progressing toward the front of the book.

Once you have finished positioning the plant on the page, place the second sheet of facial tissue or waxed paper over the plant material and close the book. This lining will assist in the drying process by absorbing moisture. Before you close the book, add bookmarks so you'll know exactly where your material is placed.

2. After you have closed the book, place additional weight on top of it. The weight can be a book of about the same size, but don't use anything too heavy, as this may crush, not flatten, the everlastings.

3. Do not disturb the pressing process for at least two weeks. Then gently open the book to the first layer to see how the drying process is progressing. If the material is still not

The large fan-shaped leaves from the ginkgo tree are paired with smaller leaves. I found both sorts of leaves on

thoroughly dry, close the book, put the additional weight back on top, and wait one more week. The process should not be hurried.

Some experts suggest you check the material several times during the pressing pro-

my walks through New York City. The backing is straw wallpaper.

cess. This additional handling is both unnecessary and potentially damaging to the plants. Dried flowers are extremely delicate; handle them as gently and infrequently as possible. It's best to leave the materials totally undisturbed and simply take extra care from the outset to make sure they are correctly positioned.

4. When the flowers and greens have dried, remove the material and store it in a flat box between tissues until you want to work with it. The materials can remain undisturbed in the box for a long time, so don't feel rushed to begin your arrangement.

5. When you're ready to assemble your design, measure the size of your frame and cut a cardboard piece to fit it—if your frame comes with a cardboard inset, you can simply use this piece. Cut your background material a ½ inch larger all around so it can be folded over and under the cardboard. Use a glue spray; be extremely careful of the placement of background material on cardboard, as the spray sets very quickly.

6. Place your pressed flowers onto their canvas with the tweezers, gently lifting and arranging them. You may even wish to sketch the placement of the flowers on a separate piece of paper beforehand so you know exactly what you want to achieve.

7. Add a small amount of glue to the background where you want to place each everlasting. Then place each everlasting on top of the glue with the tweezers. After the arrangement is done, slip it into a dust- and scratch-free frame and seal the edges with white adhesive tape. Should you use a frame that has holes punched out in the back, seal these too. Then, add a sheet of self-sealing plastic wrap to ensure that the arrangement is airtight.

CHAPTER 4

❧

POTPOURRI: RECIPES AND PRESENTATION

❧

THE WORD *POTPOURRI* COMES FROM A FRENCH term meaning "stew pot." Although this would seem to suggest a culinary substance, a potpourri is actually a fragrant mixture of any of the following: dried flowers, leaves, roots, bark, wood, spices, resins, and natural or synthetic oils.

The use of fragrances derived from flowers and oils is documented from antiquity. The floors of Cleopatra's palace were strewn with rose petals eighteen inches deep. Nero copied this practice in his palace, but also added fountains of perfume and flowers dropping from the ceilings for that special Roman panache. At Grecian banquets, hosts placed fabric containers of scented flowers in front of their guests as fragrant table favors.

Other fragrances such as incense and oils have long been used for ritual purposes in the Middle East and the Orient. Such uses were

Dried rose petals make an attractive and fragrant addition to almost any potpourri.

later adapted in the West for Christian ceremonies. People of medieval times sprinkled their floors with herbs and flowers—among them basil, lavender, rosemary, thyme, and tansy—to repel insects and deodorize the home, and sachets of potpourri were used to protect clothing from insects while also imparting a delightful scent to them. By Elizabethan times, the practice of carrying potpourri in sachet form to ward off unpleasant odors had been almost universally adopted throughout England. The Pilgrims brought this practice with them to North America.

Today, with the advertising media's emphasis on synthetic deodorizers, room-freshening sprays, scented soaps, and exotic perfumes, it is remarkable that potpourri still continues to enjoy popularity. But anyone who has ever experienced a room freshly scented with a well-blended potpourri will attest that this form of perfume remains the most honest, timeless, and delightful scent of all.

There are more than enough potpourri recipes to satisfy everyone's tastes. Ingredients can be varied to reflect the personal preferences of each individual creator. If potpourri particularly interests you and you go on to read specialized books on the topic, you will note that many of the historic recipes incorporate rose petals. In ancient times, roses were often used as decorations in both the household as well as in religious ceremonies. Greek families often grew rose-filled "gardens of Adonis"; the rose was regarded as a mystical flower in Greece, the Roman Empire, and the ancient Middle East. Egyptians would sometimes bury their dead with roses. Part of the fun of creating potpourri is incorporating the scents that delighted cultures of milleniums past.

Should you become a potpourri aficionado and want to originate your own recipes, it's wise to always have a notebook on hand to record your experiments.

Harvesting

IF YOU ARE FORTUNATE ENOUGH TO HAVE A GARden, you can create a homemade potpourri with ease. Flowers and herbs should be cut on a sunny day, after the dew has evaporated. Flowers should be in their opening stages of development; herbs should be cut right *before* they bloom because the fragrance is strongest at that time. Be sure that the specimens are healthy—the flower petals should be free of blemishes.

If you live in the city, you may want to start a window-box garden where you can grow a whole variety of small plants such as scented geraniums, lemon verbena, and a mix of herbs and wildflowers. Marigolds also dry well, though some people object to their smell. Even a large flowerpot in a sunny window will do. As the plants mature, pick a few leaves and petals each day, store them, and soon you will have enough material for a modest potpourri.

If you don't have a garden, a visit to the florist, nursery, or local market will probably turn up enough plants to use for your potpourri project.

Preserving and Drying

THE DRYING PROCESS FOR POTPOURRI IS THE same as that for everlastings used in arrangements. The only exception is that the petals are removed from the plant before drying. You may want to create a potpourri in which you use whole flowers placed on top of the mixture for display. If this is the case, do not remove the petals from the flowers when you air-dry them. Instead, cut off their stems so that about a quarter inch remains.

Place the petals or whole flowers on newspaper in the warmest, driest area available, but out of direct sunlight. Lightly cover them with newspaper or muslin, allowing enough air to circulate around the petals. Gently stir the petals and whole flowers every two or three days to prevent decay. The flowers or petals may actually dry in two to three days; however, depending on the drying environment and the amount of material, the process may take up to four weeks. Baby's breath takes only two days; whole button poms take three to four weeks. It is very important that the petals are completely dry before they are used in a potpourri because any moisture can result in mold, which will ruin the entire mixture. Make doubly sure the whole flowers are dry by checking at their centers and bases.

Herbs should be bunched up and hung to dry in a dark area. Remember that as plants dry they lose bulk, so dry enough material to allow for shrinkage. Once petals or herbs are thoroughly dried, they should be tightly sealed in labeled containers.

You need to be especially careful when choosing a container for storing your maturing potpourri. Tin boxes with tight-fitting covers are recommended because they effectively keep out light during the ripening process. Amber and green jars also work well for this reason. Mason or mayonnaise jars are also good choices because of their tight-fitting lids; however, they need to be put away in a dark place during the

process. Plastic bags can also be used for the storage of potpourri. Be sure to keep plastic out of contact with potpourri fixatives before they are mixed in, as it tends to absorb them (fixatives can actually eat through plastic). After the oils are absorbed, however, plastic containers can be used without worry.

Once you have dried your flowers, you must "season" them with a fixative. Eyedroppers are an efficient means of accomplishing this. Do not use the same eyedropper for more than one fixative; each should have a scent of its own. Eyedroppers are available in one-dram to four-ounce sizes from most drugstores and should be cleaned with rubbing or grain alcohol before their first use and between uses. It's important to follow these instructions precisely and not cut corners—the scent and purity of the fixative determines the success or failure of a potpourri.

Potpourri Ingredients

Fixatives

A FIXATIVE IS A SUBSTANCE THAT HELPS PRESERVE the delicate oils, waxes, and resins in a potpourri by extending their "shelf" lives. There are two basic categories—animal and plant. The following is a partial listing of some common fixative ingredients:

Animal

Ambergris—a solid, fatty substance expelled by sperm whales. It is often found floating on the sea or washed up on the shores of the Atlantic, the coasts of Africa, the East Indies, China, Japan, Madagascar, and the Molucca Islands. Ambergris is expensive and not available through the retail market.

Musk—an oil extracted from the scent gland of the male musk deer, which is native to China, Nepal, Siberia, and Tibet, and an essential ingredient in the manufacture of most perfumes. Since the musk deer's existence has been threatened by man's encroachment on its habitat, oil of musk is now synthesized.

Plant

Gum Benzoin—a yellowish resin produced by trees of the genus *Styrax*. Sumatra benzoin is a light brown powder available on the retail market, but is quite expensive. Compound tincture of benzoin can be purchased from your local pharmacy, has a very medicinal, spicy fragrance, and should be used sparingly in potpourri.

Orris root—a rootstock of several varieties of European irises. It exudes a delicate violet scent and is often included in potpourris that incorporate violets to highlight the fragrance, as well as others. Orris root can be purchased in powdered or cut form. The cut form is preferable, because the powdered form invariably settles to the bottom of the potpourri container.

Patchouli—an essential oil yielded by an East Indian shrubby mint. Patchouli is more often used as a scent in potpourri than as a fixative.

Sandalwood—an essential oil yielded by the heartwood of certain Indo-Malayan trees of the species *Santalum album*. It is also available in chip form.

Vetiver—an aromatic oil extracted from the roots of a grass that grows wild in Asia.

Spices

SPICES ARE VEGETABLE SUBSTANCES USED TO SEAson food and to add interesting fragrance and texture to potpourri mixtures.

Allspice—a complexly scented spice that derives from an aromatic tree that grows in the West Indies. Its odor and flavor resemble the essences of cinnamon, cloves, and nutmeg—hence, the name.

Anise—an annual aromatic herb that grows principally in Egypt. It is cultivated for its powerfully fragrant seeds, which are used both in baking and medicine, and also for crushing in potpourris.

Cinnamon sticks—a form of cinnamon derived from the bark of trees that are members of the laurel family. Cinnamon is also available in powdered and oil forms, but the sticks are fragrant and add a nice visual quality to a potpourri mixture.

Nutmeg and mace—two spices yielded from the same tree, *Myristica fragrans*, which is native to the East and West Indies, Sumatra, India, and Brazil. Mace is ground from the layer between the nutmeg shell and outer husk. The nutmeg is the nut itself, which is very dark and hard. Their pungent scents are welcome additions to a potpourri.

Tonka beans—the seeds of the tree *Dipteryxor coumarouna*, which is native to the northern areas of South America. The seed contains coumarin, which gives it an aroma similar to the vanilla bean.

Vanilla beans—beans that exude a marvelous aroma and fragrant oil. The plant is a climbing orchid native to tropical America; the oil should be used only in small amounts in potpourri.

Potpourri and pressed flower designs are romantic venues of flower craft. This charming vignette shows a small pressed flower design together with two methods for displaying potpourri: in a clear glass box and a ginger jar. The ginger jar is composed of uneven layers of bachelor's buttons, peonies, roses, and painted asters, all of which are dried in silica gel to preserve their lovely whole forms. Potpourris: Connie Wolfe

Displaying

POTPOURRI CAN BE PRESENTED IN A VARIETY OF attractive ways. Whether placed in a jar, shown off in a basket, or tied up in a sachet, this elegant form of everlastings always makes an eye-catching and fragrant display.

One popular method of displaying potpourri is to pour it into a ginger jar. The potpourri can be layered in different colors, complementing those of the room. Roses can be layered in different shades of pink and red alternated with white German or ordinary statice.

A basket can be lined with tulle, a delicate lace, or a chintz that complements the dominant colors of the potpourri. The material should be cut so that it extends slightly beyond the rim of the basket. The potpourri is then poured into the basket till it is level with the rim. To accent this design, you can arrange whole dried or pressed flowers on top of the potpourri base. During the holidays, pine cones and ribbons can also be integrated with the design.

To create a sachet, mound half a cup of potpourri into the middle of a 10-by-10-inch square of tulle. Gather the ends together and tie them closed with a 16½-inch piece of satin ribbon to make a pretty ruffle. Make the knot close to the top of the potpourri and finish with a small bow.

Culinary Potpourri

THIS BASIC MIXTURE OF FRAGRANT SPICES, FRUITS, and flowers can be created from common items found in your kitchen. The spices come from the supermarket and the compound tincture of benzoin, the glycerine, and the oil of cloves can be purchased at a drugstore. It is suggested you bring along a checklist to ensure you get all the necessary ingredients.

In addition to being easy to make, this potpourri blend is also highly adaptable. For example, pine can be added for the holiday season, while pressed and air-dried flowers can be added for show, particularly in the spring and summer months when they are most readily available. If you want to add flowers to the potpourri, avoid using white flowers (they turn brown after air-drying). The exceptions to the white flower rule are the freesia and the daisy, which can be pressed with as little stem as possible attached and added to the potpourri as a finishing touch (see general pressing instructions on pages 70-73). Choose as many varieties of the recommended flowers as you wish, in either a single or varied color scheme, and use them in whole flower form or broken up into petals. Do not overload the potpourri with flowers; allow the spices and other materials to dominate it.

With regard to your choice of ingredients, vary the proportions of spices and flowers according to your personal tastes. Use several of the spices from the supermarket, or just one or two, but not all of them together, or their fragrances will overpower one another.

Materials

glass, ceramic, or metal (*not* plastic) bowl for
  mixing;
vegetable peeler;
scissors;

small hammer (optional, used with pine
    branches);
mortar and pestle;
stainless steel spatula or spoon;
3 eyedroppers;
glass jar with tight-fitting lid for
    preservative;
tin box, mason jar, glass jar with tight-fitting
    lid, or plastic bag large enough to hold
    1 quart.

From the Drugstore:

2 ounces glycerine;
½ ounce compound tincture of benzoin;
½ ounce oil of cloves.

From the Supermarket:

1 lemon (rind);
4 oranges (rind);
1 tablespoon kosher salt (optional, for use
    with pine branches);

Choose 3 or more of the following ingredi-
    ents:

1 ounce chamomile tea leaves (loose, not tea
    bags);
1 ounce whole cloves;
1 ounce cardamom seeds;
1 ounce whole allspice;
½ ounce juniper berries;
8 cinnamon sticks;
3 medium-sized bay leaves.

From the Florist:

2 cups pine snippets (or any other greens or
    herbs);

Choose any combination of the following
    air-dried flowers with ¼-inch stem re-
    maining to make up 3 cups:

yellow or orange lilies;
yellow, red, or pink carnations;
marigolds (the odor lessens when dried);
statice (all colors);
baby's breath;
yellow button poms;
chamomile flowers.

Instructions

Preservative Mixture

1. Grate the peels of 3 oranges. Thoroughly
combine the grated peels with the glycerine,
benzoin, and oil of cloves in a glass, ceramic,
or metal bowl.

2. Transfer this mixture to a glass jar. Cover
the blend tightly and allow it to stand for 1
week in a closet or on a shelf away from light.
The mixture will not smell particularly good
at first, but will improve with age.

Potpourri

1. One day before assembling the potpourri,
remove the zest from 1 lemon and 1 orange
with a vegetable peeler and then remove the
peel itself from the fruit. Cut the peels into
thin strips and allow them to dry for a day—
they will curl as they dry. For more interesting designs, cut the pieces into fan shapes or
make curved cuts in them with scissors.

2. In a mortar, combine 3 of the supermarket ingredients that you have chosen. Crush the pieces lightly, but do not grind them to a powder. There should be some pieces left intact to provide texture and color. If you are using cinnamon sticks, use only half of them at this time.

3. Pour the mixture into your storage container, unless you are using plastic bags, in which case, pour the mixture into a glass or ceramic bowl.

4. If you are using cinnamon sticks, dip 1 end of each of the remaining cinnamon sticks into the preservative mixture. If the sticks are long, break them in half, but make sure the pieces are long enough to be recognizable in the potpourri. Add the sticks to the potpourri.

5. Add the dried lemon and orange peels to the potpourri.

6. If you are using pine, snap off small stems and gently pound them with salt using a hammer. This process releases the oil in the pine and the salt helps preserve the scent. When the stems are thoroughly treated, dip them into the preservative mixture and then add them to the potpourri. If you are using other greens, dip these into the mixture and add to the potpourri.

7. Dip the stem ends of the flowers into the preservative mixture and add them to the potpourri.

8. Gently toss the ingredients together with your hands to distribute the oils.

9. Seal the storage container. If you are using a large plastic bag or several smaller plastic bags, pour the mixture into these, but do not fill them to capacity. Allow enough room so the mixture can be gently shaken about twice a week during the 2 to 3 weeks it will need to ripen. You can gauge the progress by the potpourri's aroma. Be sure to store the mixture in a cool, dark place during this time.

These potpourris are imaginatively displayed in dried ornamental gourds that have been hollowed out.

Petal-and-Herb Potpourri

Materials

stainless steel mixing spoon;
glass, ceramic, or stainless steel measuring
  cups;
1-quart capacity glass, stainless steel, or
  ceramic mixing bowl;
eyedropper (for patchouli);
mortar and pestle;
tin box or glass jar with tight-fitting lid large
  enough to hold 1 quart.

Herbs

3 teaspoons each of up to 3 of the following:

basil;
marjoram;
mint;
rosemary;
sage;
thyme.

Fixative

1 tablespoon of 1 of the following:

patchouli;
orris root (powdered form or whole pieces
  crushed);
borax.

Spice

1 tablespoon of 1 of the following:

anise seeds;
stick cinnamon;
whole nutmeg.

Flowers

½-quart mix of 2 of the following:

larkspur delphinium;
lavender;
lily of the valley;
rose.

Instructions

1. Crumble the herbs. Mix them with the dried flowers in a bowl.

2. Add the fixative little by little until you achieve the scent strength you desire. After each bit is added, thoroughly mix the ingredients together with the mixing spoon or with your hands.

3. Crush the spices with the mortar and pestle and then add to the flower-and-herb blend.

4. Place the mixture in a labeled container, tighten the lid, and store in a cool, dark place for 4 to 6 weeks. Check on the mixture after 4 weeks to see how the fragrance has set.

Sandra Dos Passos

Another interesting method of display, this shell plate holds a potpourri of whole flowers.

CHAPTER 5

HERB GARLANDS AND WREATHS

THE HERB HAS A LONG AND VENERABLE HISTORY. Apothecary herb gardens existed for many centuries all over Europe, where the plants were cultivated for use both as flavoring agents and household curatives. In North America, the colonial "kitchen" gardens were sweet-scented places where culinary herbs such as parsley, mint, thyme, and rosemary were grown; aromatic specimens such as southernwood, borage, and hyssop were also grown in the backyard garden plot.

Interestingly, colonial Americans frequently practiced the art of drying aromatic herbs and flowers for use in sachets. Today, an herb garland is a charming way to evoke the past in addition to being a practical and convenient method of storing herbs.

Fresh herbs are often available at green grocers. Roadside stands in the country are also excellent sources. If you do purchase your herbs from a roadside stand, be prepared to keep them fresh, since a hot, dry ride in the car trunk is enough to wither them. If they do wilt on the way home despite your precautions, cut the stems diagonally, give them a little water, and they should perk right up. This is particularly true of basil.

When choosing herbs at the market, check the bunches very carefully. It is best to shop early in the morning on days when fresh stock arrives. Choose specimens with fresh green leaves; put them in a plastic bag and make sure to seal it tightly.

The herbs used in the "Herb Garland" result in a very fragrant mixture. However, feel free to substitute ingredients to create a combination that pleases you. If your garland is not for kitchen purposes, but rather for aroma, include lavender. If you wish your garland to be fuller, purchase two or three bunches of each herb. Remember that as plants dry they shrink and lose some of their bulk. Charming little Australian daisies have also been added to some of the herb bunches of this garland to make it all the more decorative. However, as with the lavender, do not add the daisies if your garland will be used in the kitchen only. Strawflowers can also be used if the garland is decorative.

Herb garlands impart a pleasurable scent and also serve as convenient all-in-one storage for kitchen ingredients. For purely decorative purposes, small bunches of flowers can be added.

Herb Garland

Materials

approximately 30 inches of supple, lightweight twine;
1 spool of fine-gauge wire;
wire cutter;
approximately 24 inches of ribbon (optional);
6 to 12 Australian daisy (or any other small
flower) clusters with 1 inch of stem remaining (if garland is decorative);

one bunch each of the following fresh herbs
with lower leaves removed:

basil,
dill,
lavender (if garland is purely for scent),
marjoram,
oregano,
sage,
tarragon,
thyme.

Instructions

1. Remove the bottom leaves from the herb
bunches so that you have more stem to work
with; the garland will be more firmly held
together this way. Grasp the end of one of
the herb bunches in one hand. In your other
hand, take wire still on the spool and wrap it
around the stem *and* the cord (approximately
3 inches down from the end of the cord).
Wrap tightly enough so that the stems are
firmly attached to the cord. Do not cut the
wire—it will run continuously along the
cord. The 3-inch area at the end of the cord is
used for grasping the garland while it is
being made and for hanging the garland.

If you wish, use only half the amount of a
particular herb in each bunch so that you can
repeat the sequence of the herbs in smaller
bunches throughout the garland. You may
also tuck a few pieces of lavender in varying
lengths into each herb bouquet or every
other bouquet. Lavender can also form its
own bouquet in the center of the garland and
different-sized clusters of Australian daisies
can be integrated into every other bouquet—
or anywhere you like in the garland.

2. Take another bunch of herbs and lay it in
the same direction as the first, overlapping
the first bunch just enough to cover the
stems. Wrap the wire firmly around the
stems and the cord 2 or 3 times.

3. Continue this process until you have used
all the bouquets but one. Attach the last one
facing in the opposite direction.

4. Cut the wire and turn it under the herbs.

5. Attach the ribbon to the other end of the
garland where there is the 3-inch piece of
cord. The ribbon ends can curl loosely along
the length of the garland. You must attach
the ribbon right away because the herbs dry
quickly—usually in about 2 days—and
should only be handled when still fresh. The
ribbon can also be attached to the 3-inch tail
and then be used to hang the garland.

6. Hang the garland to dry in the bathroom,
kitchen, or anywhere else you'd like to fill
with the marvelous fragrance of herbs.

Wreaths are appropriate for any season of the year and can be varied endlessly. This grape ivy wreath supports greens, corn husks, safflowers, and lavender.

Everlasting Herb Wreath

NOTHING LOOKS QUITE SO RUSTIC AND CHARMing as a wreath laden with herbs and flowers. In this piece, thyme, oregano, and lavender add interesting textures and scents; wispy corn husks subtly provide a sense of movement; and creamy safflowers become the focal point for the design.

A grape ivy wreath is easy to work with because it provides a natural framework in which to insert the plants. Whether the wreath you use is large or small, the process of inserting the plant material is the same. The amount of flowers, herbs, and other dried material can be varied to accommodate the size of the wreath. When choosing a wreath, make sure it is sturdily woven and there are no large spaces between the vines. If the wreath is evenly woven, insertion of material will be much easier. If you want to add a bow to the wreath, be sure to leave a predesignated opening.

In this design, the material is added a little at a time to 3 basic areas of the wreath: the upper right side; the lower right side, just to the right of the bottom center; and the lower left side. As a result, the wreath is half-filled in a kind of semicircle. The sprays of dried material extend upward on the right side and downward on the left, with everything seeming to radiate from the safflowers, although they are the last pieces to be added. This half-filled format lends the wreath a dramatic air; however, another attractive option is to make more bouquets and fill the entire wreath. As always, the choice is yours, since flower design is a very personal medium.

Remember to complete the wreath in one sitting, as the herbs dry very quickly.

Materials

grape ivy wreath, 7¾ inches in diameter;
8 three-inch picks, cut down to 2 to 2½ inches;
wire cutter;
brown floral tape;
15 to 20 stems of thyme;
10 to 15 stems of oregano;
6 to 8 corn husks, cut down to 18 slender lengths (don't cut too thin);
3 to 4 bleached safflowers;
13 stems of lavender;
glue (optional);
36 to 48 inches of ribbon.

Instructions

1. Assemble 5 bouquets composed of 3 to 4 stems of thyme and 2 to 3 stems of oregano. Attach the bouquets to picks by first holding a florist pick alongside each bouquet with its wire pointing toward the top of the bouquet. Then wrap the wire around the stems and the pick 3 or 4 times. Do not wire too tightly, but be sure that the material is securely attached and the stems lay as flat as possible on the picks. (See page 32 for instructions on wiring with picks.)

2. Wrap the brown floral tape around the stems and the pick just enough to cover the wire. (See page 32 for instructions on using floral tape.) As each pick is inserted into an opening in the vines, make sure it holds firmly—if it does not, put a few drops of glue on the wreath to hold the pick in place.

3. Add the bouquets to the wreath. Two should run along the right side pointing upward. Another should run along the bottom right corner, also pointing upward. The last 2 are located in the bottom left area and point downward.

4. Now make 3 bouquets of about 6 strips of corn husks each. Wire the picks to the centers of the strips so that they curl up on both ends.

5. Place the first bouquet on the upper right side of the wreath so that it sweeps upward with the thyme and oregano. The husks should extend beyond the wreath. Add the second bouquet slightly to the right side on the bottom of the wreath. Because the husks curl on both ends and are attached in their centers, this bouquet will point in 2 directions, following the sweep of the wreath down the left side and up the right side. Add the third bouquet to the left bottom side of the grape ivy, following its curve.

6. Next, insert individual flower stems deeply into the bottom right area of the wreath. The flowers are the highlight of this section of the grape ivy. Everything else should appear to be radiating from the flowers. If the stems do not hold, use glue to anchor them in place.

7. Finally, add the lavender to the 3 major areas of the wreath, following the lines of the other herbs. The lavender stems are strong and do not require picks for insertion. Add about 4 pieces to the upper-right area, pointing upward; about 3 pieces extending to the right of the safflowers; and approximately 6 pieces sweeping downward to the left of the safflowers. This final touch adds a spark of color and a lovely scent.

8. To hang your wreath simply loop a ribbon through it and hang it where you wish.

Displayed against a rough-hewn wall, this everlastings wreath includes wild grasses and bright touches of strawflowers.

CATALOGUE
OF MORE
EVERLASTINGS

Anthurium

Anthurium spp.

The *Anthurium* genus encompasses more than 600 species of perennial plants native to Colombia, Peru, and the West Indies. Their brilliant appearances when fresh are transformed into equally exciting forms when dry. The method used to dry them is called *watering*: Their stems are cut on a slant so they can easily absorb moisture; then they are placed in a vase containing about 2 inches of water and are left there until the flowers have dried completely. The stems are strong and the flowers hardy, although they tend to get slightly brittle. Handle them with care at all times. Unfortunately, unless you grow your own anthurium plants, the leaves are not available for drying.

Artichoke

Cynara scolymus

The artichoke is a very unusual plant. Most people are unaware that the artichoke undergoes an interesting metamorphosis if left uncut. The artichokes that arrive at the supermarket are globular forms with shiny green foliage. Those that are used in ornamental arrangements have been left to grow and develop lovely lavender and purple thistlelike flowers. These flowers dry quite nicely and retain their purple hues. Because artichoke heads are heavy, however, they require added support in an arrangement. For this reason, you must use Styrofoam as your base.

Use the watering method to dry the flower by putting the artichoke stem in 2 inches of water in a vase. This process will also take about a month, and results in the flower retaining a more vivid coloration.

Small artichokes from the supermarket take 1 month to dry. Before you hang them, cut a 7-inch piece of 28-gauge wire. Insert the wire through the stem and curl it into a U shape. Hook the two ends of wire over a hanging dowel or bar so that the artichoke hangs from it.

Australian daisy

Ixodia achilleoides compositae

Native to Australia, this wildflower's scientific name, *achilleoides*, means "yarrowlike" and refers to the plant's botanical structure. On the Australian daisy, the actual flowers are not the petals. The flowers themselves are in the center yellow area and can only be seen under extreme magnification. The flowers arrive predried and appear on the market in the fall in North America, corresponding to springtime in Australia.

The Australian daisy is an excellent flower for miniature arrangements because of its small size, and the heads, which are clusters of small flowers, can be used as filler in larger arrangements.

Bamboo

Bambusa, Arundinaria, and Dendrocalamus genera

Bamboos are actually grasses that can grow to a height of 10 stories and up to 1 foot thick. The family includes varieties that are native to many parts of the world, including the U.S., where they grow in Missouri and Maryland and as far north as Philadelphia. Southeast Asia, China, Japan, and Madagascar are also major bamboo habitats.

Bamboo is used for many purposes—in cooking, as plant supports in gardens, for furniture, and for purely decorative purposes. Marco Polo even recorded that bronze drills were rotated inside their stems to drill for oil.

You can incorporate small bamboo canes into exotic dried arrangements in many ways. One suggestion is to combine bamboo with silk Fuji mums and glycerine-treated lemon leaves (shallon). It also looks striking with dried liatris and small, dried coral-colored anthurium.

Because it is in the drying process when purchased, you can use bamboo immediately in arrangements. Some bamboo can be grown indoors and outdoors at home.

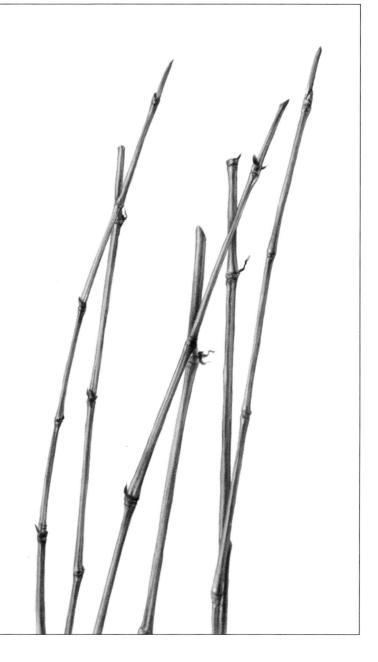

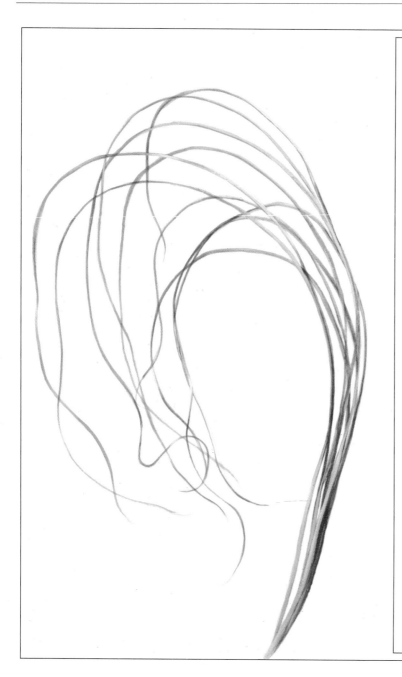

Bear grass
Xerophyllum tenax

The fire lily, *Xerophyllum tenax*, also known as bear grass, elk grass, Indian basket, and squaw grass, has white flowers and can grow up to 6 feet high, with leaves up to 3 feet long and a ½ inch wide. This plant grows from British Columbia to Wyoming and central California.

Bear grass is soft and willowy and can be dried by the watering method described in the Anthurium entry on page 96.

Bird-of-paradise

Strelitzia reginae

This much-admired plant is a perennial native of South Africa and can also be grown in California. Some species have trunks that grow to heights of 18 feet. It is a beautiful and exciting plant when fresh, with orange or yellow spikelike flowers contrasted with a dark blue stamen. When the flowers dry, however, they lose this vibrant coloring. This loss is more than compensated for by the paddle-shaped leaves, which are transformed by air drying into wonderful sculptural forms. Birds-of-paradise with the leaves still attached are hard to come by, so it is recommended that you buy more than you need when you do come across them at the florist and hang them up to dry. The stems and leaves require more than the usual amount of drying time (up to 1 month) because they are dense and retain a lot of moisture.

These extraordinary plants, handsome in flower and foliage, provide strong elements in an arrangement and lend a distinctly exotic appearance that makes them popular in contemporary-style arrangements.

Buckthorn

Rhamnus spp.

About 150 species of often thorny small trees or shrubs are in the *Rhamnus* genus. Buckthorn is chiefly grown in the temperate regions of the Northern Hemisphere, with a few grown in Brazil and South Africa. The type illustrated here is grown for its ornamental fruit. The blue-black berries that grow on buckthorn are poisonous and should be sprayed with polyurethane lacquer to ensure their hold on the branch and to give the berries an attractive shine.

To dry buckthorn, let it sit in a vase for about 3 weeks without water.

Because it is such a spectacular-looking plant, buckthorn can be used alone in a complementary vase.

Button pom
Chrysanthemum compositae

These small flowers are members of a large group of annuals and perennials that grow in the temperate and north boreal regions.

A versatile flower, the button pom dries well in silica gel in about 3 weeks' time and can also be air dried, which takes a month or more. When drying them in silica gel or any other drying agent, cut the stems to a length of 3 to 4 inches and air dry the remaining stems separately.

To dry button poms in silica gel, simply line the bottom of a good-sized box with enough drying agent so that the button poms can stand upright in it. Stand the button poms in the gel. Continue adding more silica gel—a little at a time—until the poms are lightly covered. Tap the box between additions of silica gel to distribute it evenly over the flowers.

Reattach the stems by gluing them or by wiring them to a pick. In either case, use green floral tape to cover the joint.

When air drying the flowers, hang them in small bunches with the heads pointed downward.

Caspium

Caspium; Eximium

Limonium spp.

Limonium is a genus of border perennials, biennials, or annuals. The flowers are yellowish, blue, or mauve and air dry very easily.

The most common, well-known name for this genus is statice, but its close relatives, caspia and eximium, are also excellent arranging plants.

Caspia has small, delicate flowers attached to slender stems. An excellent filler plant, it is sold predried. It is also a feathery complement to larger designs.

Eximium is native to central Asia and grows along seacoasts in the Northern Hemisphere. It, too, is available predried. Its flowers make good focal pieces in arrangements.

Eximium

Cedar roses
Pinus spp.

Many conifers drop the petals from their cones to spread seeds, leaving the base of the cone on the tree. This cone base is commonly referred to as a cedar rose, which is often sold in flower shops during the holiday season, attached to flexible wooden stems.

The cones are lovely natural ornaments in themselves, but can also be transformed by floral spray into very interesting design elements. Try spraying them with gold, silver, or any other vibrant color. They will resemble small, jeweled roses.

To increase your options, break off the wooden stem they are attached to so that it is 3 to 4 inches long. Then attach a 24- or 23-gauge wire to the remaining stem. This allows you more flexibility in designing with cedar roses because you can adjust their positions and curve them to achieve just the right line—curved or straight—in any arrangement.

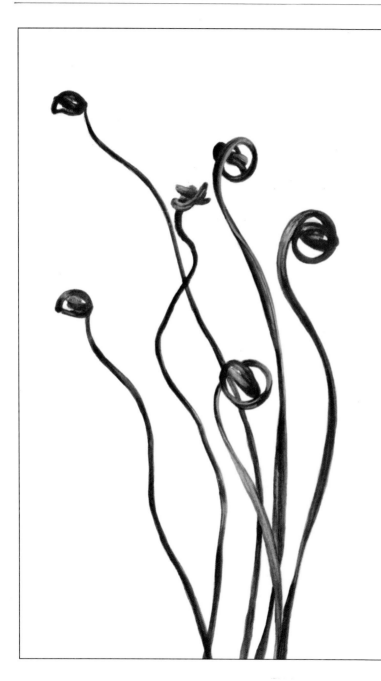

Fiddle fern, Cinnamon fern

Osmunda cinnamomea

Native to North America, the West Indies, South America, and East Asia, the fiddle fern is a highly versatile foliage plant.

The plants have a tendency to uncurl when dried; nevertheless they contribute textural interest to a design. Try spraying fiddle ferns a brilliant red with a high-gloss floral spray and then contrasting them with other, more subdued, everlastings.

Fiddle ferns can be dried by the watering method described on page 96 or hung to air dry.

Flat-leaved eucalyptus, Silver dollar

Eucalyptus polyanthemos

Eucalyptus is an important genus of sub-tropical evergreen trees of the myrtle family. They are native to Australia, Tasmania, southern Europe, and other areas where the summers are quite hot.

Eucalyptus trees yield not only valuable timber, gums, and oils but also attractive foliage that can be incorporated in any number of ways into your arrangements.

The eucalyptus illustrated here is a variety that grows in Israel. The gray-brown shade of the leaves is its natural color.

In arrangements, this species provides a lovely foliage backdrop. Because it is flat-leaved, it provides a broader coverage in arrangements.

Eucalyptus leaves can be treated with glycerine or air dried.

Galax

Galax spp.

This perennial herb is usually found in the forest. Grown in rock gardens, it is a good ground cover. The delicate white flowers that appear on the plant in the spring and shade to bronze in the fall make galax an attractive plant from season to season. Only the leaves, however, are available at the florist.

For use in dried arrangements, galax can be pressed or treated with glycerine. When the foliage is pressed, a 3-inch stem should be left.

When using the glycerine treatment, cut the stem to a 3-inch length after the process. Attach the leaf to a 3-inch wooden pick and tape the joint with floral tape for use in arrangements.

The galax leaf is a lovely covering material in arrangements and will serve the twofold purpose of camouflaging foam and providing an attractive accent.

Gladiolus leaves

Gladiolus spp.
G. byzantinus, G. communis,
G. primulinus, etc.

Approximately 300 species are members of the *Gladiolus* genus. The plants are chiefly from Africa and have erect, sword-shaped leaves. Their genus name refers to the Latin word *gladius,* or sword. Grown both commercially and in private gardens, gladiolus plants yield many interesting foliage varieties that can be used in a number of ways in arrangements.

One of the best features of gladiolus leaves is their sturdiness. Because they are so strong, they can be manipulated in a variety of ways in a design. When dried, they curl and twist in shapes that accentuate their distinctive length. Although some dried gladiolus leaves retain their green coloration, the majority turn a golden yellow, sometimes striped with green. Either way, they make handsome additions to arrangements.

Gladiolus leaves will dry with a little bit of water in a vase in about a week or less for smaller leaves. Larger plants may require 2 to 3 weeks to dry. When inserting the stems into foam, cut them on a slant so that they can be inserted easily.

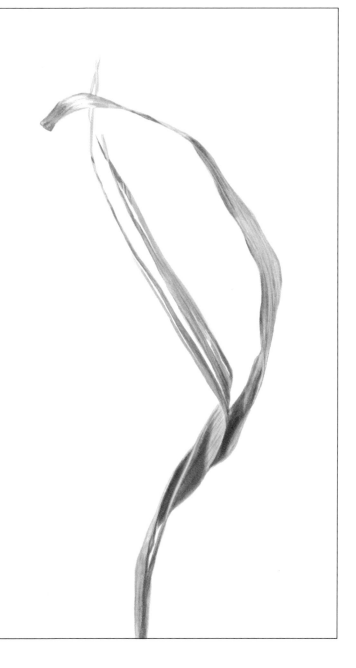

Crown gourd

Warty gourd

Crookneck gourd

Squash gourd

Gourds

Cucurbita, Lagenaria genera

The gourd is a hard-rinded, inedible fruit that is often used for ornament, vessels, and utensils. The *Lagenaria* genus consists of the flowerlike variety; the *Cucurbita* genus encompasses many shapes and sizes including globular, oblong, cylindrical, club shaped, dumbbell shaped, and crooknecked.

Purchase gourds well in advance of their planned use in an arrangement. Gourds take a long time to dry—depending on the size, 3 to 4 months. Wash them off, dry them, and then spray them with any household disinfectant. To accelerate the drying process, pierce the bottom and top of each gourd with a poultry skewer (lacer) to provide ventilation. The holes need not be very deep or large. If you want the gourds to stand upright, pierce holes only in the bottoms so that the tops will appear smooth.

For gourds with necks, tie strings around the necks and hang them up to dry in a shaded place. For those that cannot be hung up, place them on a rack—such as the kind used for cooling breads and cakes—in a shaded location and turn them several times during the drying process. If any film or mold appears on the gourds, wash it off with soap and water. Be prepared for some losses, as gourds do not always dry well. You'll know a gourd is completely dry when the seeds inside it rattle. Sometimes a freckled or petaled pattern will appear on a gourd. To further enhance your gourds after they've dried, they can be polished with floor wax or coated with polyurethane lacquer in matte or high gloss. Beware of the preglazed gourds on the market: These tend to rot quickly and can only be used for temporary arrangements.

Grevillea
Grevillea spp.

A native of Australia and New Caledonia, and now grown in California, this member of the protea family has leaves that are red, mauve, yellow, blue, or orange on top and silvery-gray underneath. It dries easily by the watering method described on page 96. As they dry, the leaves take on beautiful curls.

Striking in color, grevillea works wonderfully by itself in a free-form arrangement or as a filler in a piece that requires a distinctive color accent.

Hakea, Cup plant
Hakea spp.

Members of the protea family, hakeas comprise between 130 and 140 species of evergreen shrubs and small trees native to Australia, Tasmania, and South Africa. They can also be grown in parts of California and are able to withstand a slight frost.

The leaves are positioned on the stem in such a way that they resemble a cup, hence one of its common names. They develop small pink or white flowers.

Hakeas are available commercially dried. Use them in arrangements with very strong, bold designs.

Heliconia

Heliconia rostrata

A tropical plant with large bananalike leaves and brilliant flowers arranged in boat-shaped bracts, heliconia is an excellent choice for use in a dramatic design.

Heliconia rostrata can be hand painted when dried to revive some of the brilliant color the plant possesses when fresh. A final glossy coating of polyurethane spray makes them particularly attractive in an arrangement. They take 2 to 3 weeks to air dry and are attractive display plants even while drying because of their unusual forms. The specimen illustrated here is in the process of drying.

Heliconia may also be dried using the watering method described on page 96.

Honey-locust pods

Gleditsia triancanthos

Honey-locust trees grow widely throughout North America in both the country and the city. Because of their wide availability, honey-locust pods are a natural choice for dried designs.

The pods have interesting sculptural qualities that can be utilized in many ways in a dried arrangement. The "Autumn Basket" arrangement on page 59 is just one example of how it can be used.

Generally, honey-locust pods are quite strong and can easily be inserted into foam. If you are using Styrofoam, however, you will need to cut an 8-inch length of 28-gauge wire; insert it into the pod in a flat area that does not contain seed; fold the wire down and twist the two ends together to form a strong 4-inch stem.

Horsetails

Equisetum spp.
E. hyemale, E. arvense,
E. scirpoides, etc.

These marsh plants are related to ferns and grow along river edges and in wetland areas of North America, Europe, and Asia. The Latin name is derived from the words *equus*, horse, and *seta*, bristle.

These flowerless species are used as both ornamental garden plants and as attractive additions to arrangements. Horsetails can be used like bamboo in everlastings designs, since its clean, straight lines make interesting counterpoints to rounded flower shapes.

Horsetails can also be manipulated to form zigzags and other shapes by inserting a wire through its stem and bending it into the desired position.

These plants can be grown in the home garden. They dry very quickly when left in a vase, without water, for a few days.

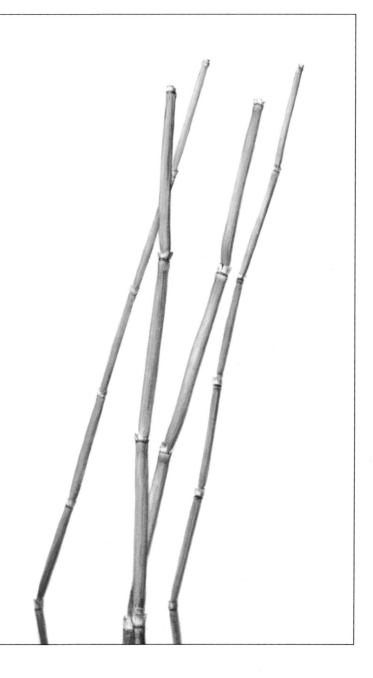

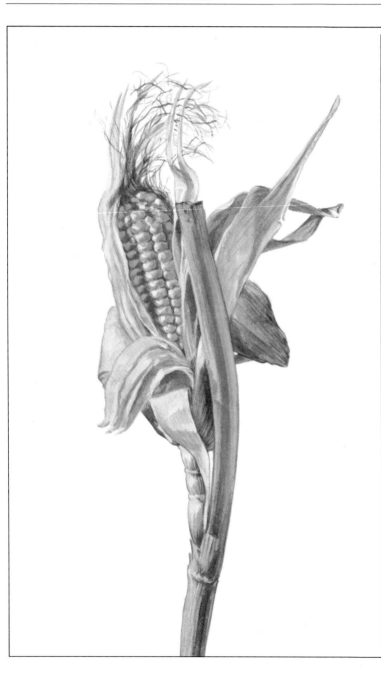

Indian corn, Zea

Zea mays

Indian corn is a member of a genus of annual grasses that is used as fodder grain for horses. The plant is not known in the wild as the wild parent species is long extinct. The Indian corn we know is a descendant of the kinds of corn grown by Indians when Europeans first arrived in the New World.

The grains come in white, yellow, red, and black and the plants may grow to a height of 15 feet.

This type of corn is used widely as a dried ornamental and can act as a focal point for autumn designs.

Kangaroo paw

Anigozanthos spp.
A. coccineus, A. flavidus,
A. humilis, etc.

There are 10 perennial herbs in the *Anigozanthos* genus. They have thick rootstocks and are native to southwestern Australia, but can also be grown in southern California. Kangaroo paws dry very well but require careful handling, as the flowers detach very easily. The most common colors available are yellow, purple, and variegated yellow and brown varieties. The purple flowers dry to an almost black color.

The leaves of these plants are either linear or sword shaped, but because they become too brittle when dry, they cannot be used in dried arrangements.

The flowers can be dried by the watering method (see page 96). This process generally takes a week and a half.

The yellow kangaroo paw flowers are particularly nice in many arrangements because they provide bright spots of color.

Lemon leaf, Shallon

Gualtheria spp.

Not to be mistaken for the foliage of the common lemon tree, the greens illustrated are grown in the subtropical regions of Asia, Australia, and the Americas, from Canada to Chile. The plants are grown for many purposes: They yield fruits, flowers, and outstanding evergreen foliage.

The leaves can be dried using the glycerine treatment. Use them in dramatic, large-scale arrangements.

Leucodendron

Leucodendron spp.

A member of the protea family, this genus encompasses about 60 species of trees and shrubs that can be grown in North America. All leucodendrons have male and female flowers on separate plants. Particularly nice in autumn pieces, the leucodendron's interesting leaves as well as its unusually structured flower head make it a very distinctive flower in arrangements. Try using it with other dried material of equally unusual form, pieces like the fan palm or the curly willow.

Leucodendron should be air dried prior to use.

Leucodendron silignum

Leucodendron glabrum

Lycopodium, Club moss

Lycopodium spp.
L. cernuum, L. clavatum, etc.

The genus name of this unusual plant is derived from the Greek word *lykos* (wolf) and *podion* (foot). The genus encompasses over 450 species of evergreen perennial herbs of wide geographic distribution. Often included in dried designs is *L. cernuum*, a native of Hawaii, which is frequently used as a Christmas green. By contrast, *L. clavatum*—sometimes called running pine— is native to North America, Europe, and temperate Asia. Its stems arch dramatically and the plant may grow to several feet in length.

Lycopodium is used as a filler plant in arrangements, lending interesting touches while not dominating the design. Because it is a good holiday green, try mixing it with holly, berries, and pine cones. In the springtime, lycopodium contrasts well with delicate flowers. Its unusual branches also form a nice complement to contemporary designs.

To dry lycopodium, air dry it in a vase or hung upside-down, or treat it with glycerine.

Minicarnations

Dianthus spp.

Perhaps originally a native of the Mediterranean region, carnations are now cultivated all over the world for their use in perfumes and versatility as cut flowers. Carnations have been cultivated for over 2,000 years; modern varieties bloom over a long period of time and provide large numbers of splendid blooms in many colors and combinations, among them red, magenta, white, yellow-orange, and variegated. New varieties are produced regularly. The minicarnations illustrated here are lovely examples of the diversity of forms a carnation can take: Many flowers grow on shoots off of one stem. Propagation of carnations for window boxes or greenhouses is done by taking cuttings from the strong shoots that rise from the base of the plant, rooting them in sand, and potting them.

Dry minicarnations with silica gel, following the instructions on page 103. They will take only about 3 days to dry.

Golden mushroom

Mushrooms— Golden mushroom, Sponge mushroom

Polyporus perennis, Coriolus versicolor

Mushrooms are found in temperate climates in all parts of the world. They grow wild in pastures, lawns, and woodlands—anywhere the ground is enriched by manure or humus. Mushrooms are also a common sight on tree stumps and logs.

The two specimens illustrated are the golden mushroom—*Polyporus perennis*—and the sponge mushroom—*Coriolus versicolor*. Both are available commercially dried. The golden mushroom is inedible, but quite useful in everlastings arrangements as a very earthy-looking accent.

The sponge mushroom is also inedible. It is found growing on the decaying wood of broad-leaved trees. Because it dries well, it is another excellent choice for everlastings designs. Its shelflike shape—with interesting textures—can be dramatically contrasted with other unusual shapes, such as those of artichokes and protea, to create a very bold design.

Sponge mushroom

Inflorescence of palm

Easter palm

Palm

Palma spp.

The palm is an outstanding decorative evergreen. Grown in greenhouses and arboretums and planted in tropical and temperate areas throughout the world, the palm is an important plant that yields many products such as oils and coconuts.

Palms are named for the formation of their leaves, because they grow in a hand-like or "palm" shape. The lore of this ancient plant goes back to early history when the palm was used in processions to symbolize triumph and joy.

Some palms, such as the Easter palm, can be press-dried while others, such as the canary palm, should be allowed to air dry in fine curls. Both processes take only a few days. Palms can generally be manipulated into many shapes.

Also available for drying is the inflorescence of the palm (see illustration at left). This is the greenery that is left after the fruit of the palm has dropped.

Because palms for the most part have strong stems, they can be inserted directly into foam.

Use palms as greens to contrast against flowers or as a covering and filler in arrangements.

Canary palm

Papyrus
Cyperus papyrus

Papyrus was the ancient writing paper of Egypt, Palestine, Syria, and southern Europe. The paper scrolls were made by pressing together strips of pith from the stems while the plant was still wet. Today, however, this tender aquatic is used primarily as an ornamental plant.

Papyrus can be grown as a potted plant in the home. A small 3-inch specimen can easily grow to 6 feet over several years.

Papyrus is commercially treated with glycerine and sometimes dyed green. It is usually available in 12-inch lengths.

Because papyrus is often precut, you may want to lengthen the stem by gluing a garden support or dowel—painted the same color as the papyrus—to the stem and sealing the joint with green floral tape. Use it with other greens, such as palm, to camouflage the support.

Papyrus also looks wonderful when combined with artificial silk flowers.

Podocarpus, Southern yew

Podocarpus spp.
P. macrophyllus, P. nagi, P. neriifolius, etc.

About 75 species of coniferous shrubs and trees are members of the *Podocarpus* genus. Native to the temperate Southern Hemisphere and to the mountains and highlands of the tropics, and north to the West Indies, Japan, and North America, podocarpus do not on first inspection look like conifers. They have flat and sometimes broad leaves, which make them a unique-looking evergreen.

The name *Podocarpus* comes from the Greek *podos* (foot) and *karpos* (fruit) and refers to their often thick, fleshy fruit stalks. Podocarpuses are of ancient lineage, closely related to species that were once abundant nearly 200 million years ago.

P. nagi is often used in bonsai designs. Popular arrangement varieties include *P. macrophyllus* and *P. neriifolius,* the latter most often seen as a decorative plant.

Podocarpus can be air dried or preserved using glycerine. Its reaction to glycerine is sometimes quite striking, as the plant may become striated with red and yellow hues.

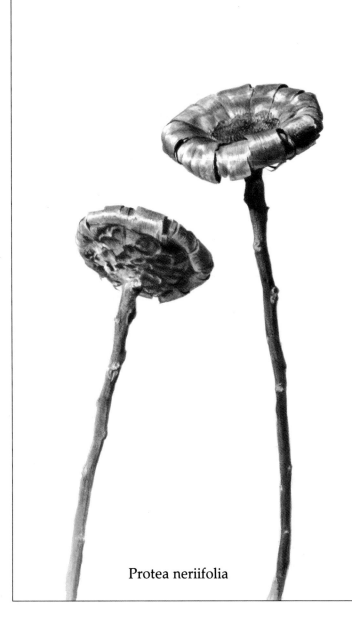

Protea neriifolia

Protea

Protea spp.
P. compacta, P. neriifolia, etc.

The name protea is an allusion to the Greek god Proteus, who possessed the ability to assume many forms. The name is fitting, for the protea genus includes approximately 130 species of African and Australian shrubs and small trees, and encompasses many other families including hakea, grevillea, and leucodendron (see individual entries).

Available predried, protea takes many forms, but the kinds most often used in dried arrangements have large heads covered with richly colored flowers ranging in color from salmon pink to carmine.

P. compacta is a branched shrub that grows up to 10 feet high. Its leathery leaves are 4 or more inches long.

P. neriifolia, also known as pink mink and oleander-leaved protea, can grow to heights of 6 feet. The specimen illustrated here has gone to seed; the bracts have dropped, leaving modified leaves which have reflexed back to give the flower its daisy-petal look.

Protea compacta

Bottle brush protea

Ranunculus

Ranunculus spp.
R. asiaticus, R. acontifolius,
R. Ragionieri, etc.

Approximately 50 species of ranunculus grow around the world, in the Russian Caucasus, Canada, Greenland, Alaska, and much of the United States. The specimen illustrated here is *R. Ragionieri*. They have a short season on the market in the springtime, so it's important to buy them when available and dry and store them for future use.

To dry ranunculus, cut the stems to 3- or 4-inch lengths. Insert them in a 1-inch high piece of Styrofoam that fits the bottom of the box and has been attached to it with glue. Make sure the heads do not touch the top of the box. Cover the flowers lightly with silica gel, adding a little at a time and tapping lightly as you progress to distribute the gel. They require approximately 3 days to dry.

If you want taller flowers but don't want the heads to droop, run a 28- or 26-gauge wire up the stem, but not into the head.

Red bottlebrush
Callistemon

A native of southeastern Australia, this unusual, thistlelike plant can also be found growing in the midwestern plains areas of North America. The crimson flowers provide attractive bursts of color in a design.

Red bottlebrush can be purchased in predried form or can be bought fresh and air dried. It will look lovely mixed with bold greens or as the focal point of a minimal design.

Ruscus

Ruscus
Ruscus spp., esp. *R. aculeatus*

Ruscus is an evergreen shrub that is a native of Western Europe and the Mediterranean region. The leaves are actually branchlets, that is, a branch that resembles an ordinary foliage leaf. It is the interesting quality of ruscus leaves that makes them such an intriguing green to work with in arrangements. Ruscus is grown in the U.S. and is widely available in florist shops. Florists frequently use dried, artificially colored sprays of ruscus in autumn and winter arrangements.

Treat ruscus with glycerine before use. It can also be air dried.

Dyed ruscus (different species)

Verticordia

Verticordia nitens

The Latin word *monadelpha* refers to plants with stamens that are combined to form one piece, as in the mallow family. Golden morrison is also a monadelpha, as is this very delicate, pink woolly flower from the verticordia shrub that is native to south-western Australia.

The flowers are yellow, red, or scarlet. When they arrive on the market, they are already dried and ready to use in any number of interesting ways. Because it is such a small flower, try using it in miniature arrangements.

White daisy

Layia glandulosa

This very popular little flower has a long growing season and dries very well in silica gel. (The procedure for drying flowers in silica gel is described on page 103.)

Allow 2 to 3 days to dry. Check for dryness by carefully uncovering one flower. The daisy should feel papery dry.

Afterword

NOT EVERYONE WHO READS *EVERLASTING Design* will become a devotee of dried-flower arrangements, but it is hoped that this book will add another dimension to your appreciation of not only dried but fresh and silk flowers. Flower arranging is a personal art that can reflect your choices in style in both your home and office. It is an art form that can improve the aesthetic quality of your everyday life while also offering a creative outlet and sense of accomplishment. While it is relaxing, it is also exciting in that with just a few tools and a few flowers you can create an original arrangement.

To those of you who have been inspired to become further involved in this very interesting and rewarding activity, I suggest you learn more about dried-flower arranging in all its modes: traditional, Ikebana, and the like. Consult the bibliography of this volume for books that provide information on a variety of subjects. You might also wish to take flower-arranging classes. Many horticultural societies and botanical gardens offer such classes to members and nonmembers.

Don't be afraid to experiment with plant materials that you think might dry well. There are many kinds I was unable to represent in this book, so it is up to you to experiment with flowers and greens that are regionally available. As this book has stressed, be curious and adventurous in your choice of materials and designs. In doing so, you will develop your own style. That is what this book is all about: you and your personal approach to flowers. You'll find that as you work with these materials, your mind and eye will become increasingly better trained to discover the hidden possibilities of floral designing. A whole world of enjoyment awaits you.

BIBLIOGRAPHY

Arranging and Flower Craft

Aaronson, Marian. *The Art of Flower Arranging*. London: Grower Books, 1975. (Distributed in the U.S. by ISBS Inc., P.O. Box 555, Forest Grove, OR 97116.)

Burnett, Kay. *Ikebana Collection: Studies in Sogetsu Ikebana*. New York: Van Nostrand Reinhold, 1979.

Cook, Hal. *Arranging: The Basics of Contemporary Flower Design*. New York: William Morrow, 1985.

Davidson, Georgie. *Classical Ikebana: The Japanese Art of Flower Design*. New York: A.S. Barnes & Co., 1970.

Dutton, Joan Parry. *Colonial Williamsburg Decorates for Christmas*. New York: Holt, Rinehart and Winston by arrangement with the Colonial Williamsburg Foundation, 1981.

_____. *The Flower World of Williamsburg*. New York: Holt, Rinehart and Winston by arrangement with the Colonial Williamsburg Foundation, 1973.

Ingham, Vicki I. *Elegance in Flowers: Classic Arrangements for All Seasons*. Birmingham, AL: Oxmoor House, 1985.

Loring, John and Henry B. Platt. *New Tiffany Table Settings*. Garden City, NY: Doubleday, 1981.

MacQueen, Sheila. *Flowers and Food for Special Occasions*. London: Hyperion, 1980.

Madderlake, Tom, et al. *Flowers Rediscovered: New Ideas for Using and Enjoying Flowers*. New York: Stewart, Tabori & Chang, 1985.

Otis, Denise and Maia Ronaldo. *Decorating With Flowers*. New York: Abrams, 1981.

Pearson, Katherine. *Nature Crafts*. Birmingham, AL: Oxmoor House, 1980.

Webb, Iris, ed. *The Complete Guide to Flower and Foliage Arrangement*. Garden City, NY: Doubleday, 1982.

Dried Flowers

Mierhof, Annette. *The Dried Flower Book: Growing, Picking, Drying, Arranging*. New York: E.P. Dutton, 1981.

Thorpe, Patricia. *Everlastings: The Complete Book of Dried Flowers*. New York: Facts on File, 1985.

Gardening

Dietz, Marjorie A. *The ABCs of Gardening Outdoors and Indoors*. New York: W.H. Smith Publishers, 1979.

Readers Digest Editors. *Illustrated Guide to Gardening*. New York: Random House, 1978.

Taylor, Patricia. *The Weekender's Gardening Manual*. New York: Holt, Rinehart and Winston, 1986.

Yang, Linda. *The Terrace Gardener's Handbook*. Portland, OR: Timber Press, 1975.

History and Reference

The American Horticultural Society. *N.A. Horticulture Guide*. New York: Scribner's, 1985. (A handbook of horticultural organizations, plant societies, educational programs, public gardens, scholarly organizations, botanical and horticulture libraries, conservation groups, and garden club associations.)

Crowell, Robert L. *The Lore and Legends of Flowers*. New York: Crowell Books, 1982.

Hay, Roy, et al. *The Dictionary of Indoor Plants*. New York: Exeter Books by special arrangement with The Royal Horticultural Society, 1983.

Potpourri and Pressed Flowers

Fettner, Ann Tucker. *Incense and Other Fragrant Concoctions*. New York: Workman Publishing, 1977.

Gruenberg, Louise. *Potpourri: The Art of Fragrance Crafting*. Norway, IA: Frontier Cooperative Herbs, 1984.

USEFUL ADDRESSES

Instruction

American Floral Art School
539 South Wabash
Chicago, IL 60605

Atlanta Botanical Garden
Box 77246
Atlanta, GA 30357

Brooklyn Botanical Garden
1000 Washington Avenue
Brooklyn, NY 11225

California Arboretum Foundation
& L.A. State & County Arboretum
301 North Baldwin Avenue
Arcadia, CA 91006–2697

Chicago Botanic Garden
P.O. Box 400
Glencoe, IL 60022
(course guides issued three times a year)

Floral Design School
State University of New York
Continuing Education & Public Service
Agricultural & Technical College
Cobleskill, NY 12043

Floro Video
"Flower Arranging is for Everyone"
P.O. 281
Needham, MA 02134
(video instruction)

Garden Club of America
598 Madison Avenue
New York, NY 10022
(provides directories of garden clubs
throughout the U.S.; check listings for
flower-arranging instruction)

Missouri Botanical Garden
4344 Shaw Boulevard
St. Louis, MO 63110

The New York Botanical Garden
Education Department
Bronx, NY 10458
(commercial flower-arranging instruction)

Pennsylvania Horticultural Society
325 Walnut Street
Philadelphia, PA 19106
(classes offered to members)

School of Floral Design
3106 West Avenue
San Antonio, TX 78213

Periodicals

Harrowsmith
Camden House
The Creamery
Charlotte, VT 05445
(published bimonthly; information on
gardening and crafts)

Herb Basket
P.O. 1773
Brattleboro, VT 05301
(published bimonthly; information on
growing plants for food and decoration)

Plant and Equipment Supplies

Galerie Felix Flower
968 Lexington Avenue
New York, NY 10021
(dried materials)

Le Jardin du Gourmet
Box 72
West Danville, VT 05873
(carries special seed mixes for small
gardens, indoor and patio gardens)

Beatrice Mann Florist
116 Central Park South
New York, NY 10019
(dried, special order only)

People's Flowers Corporation
786 Sixth Avenue
New York, NY 10001
(dried materials and supplies)

Plantabbs Corporation
P.O. Box 397
Timonium, MD 21093
(silica gel)

Rialto Florist Inc.
707 Lexington Avenue
New York, NY 10022
(dried materials)

Richard Salome Flowers
152 East 79th Street
New York, NY 10021
(dried, special order only)

Twigs
399 Bleecker Street
New York, NY 10014
(dried, special order only)

Van Bourgondien Brothers
Box A
Route 109
Babylon, NY 11702
(free catalog)

INDEX

Page numbers in italics refer to captions and illustrations.

Acacia, 68
Achilleoides, 98
Allspice, 79
Alyssum, 68
Amaranthus, *60–61, 62-63*
Ambergris, 78–79
Anchoring: materials for, 24–26
Anigozanthos spp., 117
Anise, 79
Anthurium spp., *33,* 96
Arborvitae, 68
Arrangement techniques, 32–38
Artichokes, *27,* 97
Arundinaria spp., 99
Asters, *80*
Australian daisies, 98

Baby's breath, 30, 31, 66, 78
Bachelor's buttons, *80*
Bamboo, 99
Bambusa spp., 99
Banksia attenuata, 9
Bar-fast, 24
Basil, 69, 77, 88
Baskets, 15, *16–17*
Bear grass, *38,* 100
Bending, 32–34
Benzoin, 79, 81
Bird-of-paradise, 101
Bittersweet, 15, *16–17,* 30
Black-eyed Susans, 31
Bowls: oval, 19
Branches, 12, 30, *37;* curving of, 32–34
Brown foam, 15, *17,* 24
Brushes, 23
Buckthorn, *38–39,* 102
Button poms, 78, 103

Cactus, 68
Callistemon, 131
Camouflaging of foams, 26–28
Campanulas, 56, *57*
Capucin leaves, *20*
Carnations, 68
Caspium, 104
Cats: mixture to repel, 23

Cedar roses, *17, 35,* 105
Ceramics, 13, *21*
Chrysanthemum compositae, 103
Cinnamon, 79
Cinnamon ferns, 106
Cities: specimen collecting in, 7–8, 28–30
Clematis, 31
Clover, 30, 66, 68
Cloves, 69, 81
Club moss. *See* Lycopodium
Containers, 13–19
Coreopsis, 68
Coriander, 69
Coriolus versicolor. See Mushrooms
Corn, *60–61, 62-63, 90–91,* 116
Cornflowers, 31
Cosmos, 31, 66
Coxcomb, *18*
Crystal, 13
Cucurbita. See Gourds
Cup plant, 112
Curly willow, 12
Curving, 32–34
Cynara scolymus. See Artichokes
Cyperus papyrus, 126

Daisies, *17,* 30, 31, *37,* 66, 67, 68, 81, 88, 98, 135
Delphinium, 30, *38,* 56
Dendrocalamus spp., 99
Dianthus spp. *See* Minicarnations
Dill, *14, 35*
Dipteryxor coumarouna, 79
Dismantling arrangements, 38
Dock, *41*
Driftwood, *30*
Drying process: for potpourri, 77–78

Echinops, *21*
Elk grass, 100
Equisetum spp., 115
Eucalyptus spp., *7, 27, 36,* 107
Everlastings (Thorpe), 30
Eximium, *25,* 104

Ferns, 28, 66, 106
Fiddle ferns, 106
Fixatives: for potpourri, 78–79
Florist picks, 22

Florists: specimens purchased from, 28–30
Foam. *See* Bar-fast; Brown foam; Styrofoam
Freesia, *38*, 81
Fresh materials: dried materials mixed with, 56–59
Freshness: steaming for, 34
Fuchsia, 31

Galax spp., 28, 108
Gardenias, 67
Garlands, 86–93
Geraniums, 66, 69, 77
Gerbera daisy, 56
German statice. *See* Statice
Ginkgo leaves, *72–73*
Gladiolus spp., *41*, 109
Glass, 15
Gleditsia triancanthos. See Honey-locust pods
Glue, 22
Glycerine, 23, 28, 30, 81: treatment of leaves using, *7*
Golden mushrooms. *See* Mushrooms
Goldenrod, 31
Gourds, *8, 9, 20, 26–27, 59–63, 83*, 110
Grevillea spp., *14, 26–27, 29*, 111
Gruenberg, Louis, 66
Gualtheria. See Lemon leaves
Gypsophilia, 31

Hafner, Dorothy, *29*
Hakea spp., *27*, 112
Heliconia spp., 15, 36, 113
Henry's foam. *See* Brown foam
Herbs: in garlands and wreaths, 86–93; *See also specific herbs*
Holiday designs, 48–53
Holly, *17*, 30, *40, 50, 51, 52*, 60
Honey-locust pods, *60–61, 62–63*, 114
Hops, 30
Horsetails, 115
Hyacinth, 30
Hydrangea, 30
Hystrix patula, *34–35*

Ikebana (design type), *25*, 34, 53–56
Illium, *66, 67*
Indian basket, 100
Indian corn, 116
Irises, 53, *54*, 79
Ivy, 28, 31, 56, 66, 69, *90–91*
Ixodia achilleoides compositae, 98

Jack-o-lanterns, *16–17*
Jonquil, 69

Kangaroo paw, 117

Kenzan, 24–26
Knives, 22
Kraynek-Prince, Fran, *16–17*

Lagenaria. See Gourds
Larkspur, 69
Lavender, 31, *46*, 48, 77, 88, *90–91*
Layia glandulosa, 135
Lemon leaves, *14*, 27, 28, *28–29*, *41*, 56, *60–61*, 118
Lemon verbena, 31, 77
Leucodendron, 119
Leucodendron spp., *28–29*, 119
Liatris, 30, *41*, 56
Lilacs, 69
Limonium spp., 104
Linen pods, *40, 50, 51, 52*
Lycopodium spp., 44, *46*, 48, 120

Mace, 79
Marigolds, 77
Marjoram, 31, 69
Minicarnations, *38*, 121
Minigladiolas, 56, *57*
Mint, 69
Morrison flowers, 60, *60–61*
Moss. *See* Lycopodium; Spanish moss; Sphagnum moss
Mushrooms, *27*, 60, *60-61*, 122–23
Musk, 79
Myristica fragrans, 79

Narcissus, 31
Nasturtium, 31
Nero, 75
Nutmeg, 79
Nyburg, Mary, *37*

Oak leaves, *60–61*
Orchids, 67
Orris root, 79
Osmunda cinnamomea. See Ferns
Oval bowls, 19

Packing, 12
Painting, *18*, 34–36, 71
Palm, *14*, 69, 124–25
Palma spp., 124–25
Pansies, 31, 67, 69
Papyrus, 126
Parsley, 31, 69
Patchouli, 79
Pearly white everlastings, 49, *50*, 60
Peonies, 30, *80*
Philodendrons, 56, 66

Pine, *17,* 69, 81
Pine cones, 30, *40, 50, 51, 52,* 60, 81
Pine needles, *16–17, 40*
Pinus spp. *See* Cedar roses
Pittosporum, 56, 57
Podocarpus spp., *6, 7, 8, 9, 27,* 127
Poinsettia, *17,* 40
Polo, Marco, 99
Polyporus perennis. See Mushrooms
Polysilk holly, *17,* 40
Potpourri: The Art of Fragrance Crafting (Gruenberg), 66
Potpourris, 74–85
Preservation: for potpourri, 77–78
Preservatives, 23
Pressed flowers, 64–73
Prince, Neil, *16–17*
Protea spp., *9, 14, 27, 28–29, 34–35, 41,* 128–29
Pussy willow, 12, *14,* 34, 56, *57*

Queen Anne's lace, 66, *67*

Ranunculus spp., *6, 7,* 69, 130
Red bottlebrush, 131
Rhamnus spp. *See* Buckthorn
Rhododendron, 7
Rosemary, 31, 77
Roses, *17,* 35, 69, 76, 77, *80,* 81, 105
Rulers, 22
Ruscus spp., *18, 20, 25, 26–27, 27,* 28, *41,* 56, 132–33

Safflowers, *41, 90–91*
Sage, 69
Sahara, 15, 24
"Salad of the desert," *67*
Salvia, *17*
Sandalwood, 79
Santalum album, 79
Sea shells, 30
Shadow, Harvey, *33*
Shallon. *See* Lemon leaves
Shokotu (Japanese nobleman), 53
Silica gel, 23, *38;* drying with, *6, 7*
Silver lace, 30
Southern yew, 127
Spanish moss, *6, 7, 14, 19, 20,* 44, *55;* as camouflage for foam, 26–28
Sphagnum moss, 28
Spices: in potpourri, 79
Spider mums, 56, *57*
Sponge mushrooms. *See* Mushrooms
Sprays, 23
Squaw grass, 100
Starfish, *30*

Statice, *6, 7, 26–27,* 30, *40, 45, 46,* 48, 81
Steaming, 32–34
Stems: wiring of, 32
Storage, 12–13
Strawflowers, *37, 46,* 48, 60, *60–61,* 88, *92–93*
Strelitzia spp., *21,* 101
Styrax, 79
Styrofoam, 14, 15, 19, 24, 27, 35, 39; camouflaging of, 26–28
Sunflowers, 69
Sweet basil, 69, 77, 88
Sweet William, 31
Sycamore pods, *40*

Tansy, *41,* 77
Tape, 23
Tarragon, 31
Terra-cotta plant saucers, 13
Thomas, Byron, *9*
Thorpe, Patricia, 30
Thyme, 31, 77
Tonka beans, 79
Tools, 22–23
Torrey pine needles, *16–17*
Traditional arrangements, 44–48
Transporting of arrangements, 38–39
Tulips, 56
Tweezers, 23

Vanilla, 79
Verticordia spp., *37,* 134
Vetiver, 79
Violets, *67,* 69, 79

Watercolors, 22
Wheat, *41, 60–61, 62–63,* 69
White daisies, 135
Wild grass, *92–93*
Willow, 12, *14,* 34, *41,* 53, 56, *57*
Window boxes, 31
Wire, 22
Wire cutters, 22
Wiring, 32
Wolfe, Connie, *80*
Work space, 12–13
Wreaths, 86–93

Xerophyllum tenax, 100

Yellow button poms, *8, 9*

Zea, 116
Zea mays, 116
Zinnias, 69